THE EPISTLES OF HORACE

THE

EPISTLES

OF HORACE

DAVID FERRY

FARRAR, STRAUS AND GIROUX

NEW YORK

Farrar, Straus and Giroux

Printed in the United States of America
First edition, 2001

The following epistles have previously appeared in and are reprinted with the permission of Arion *(i.7, i.12, i.13, i.19)*, Literary Imagination: The Review of the Association of Literary Scholars and Critics *(i.16)*, Persephone *(i.5, i.8)*, Slate *(i.15), and* TriQuarterly Review *(a publication of Northwestern University) (part of i.1, i.10, i.20).*

The Latin text used here is from Q. Horati Flacci. Opera. *Ed. Shackleton Bailey. 3rd ed. Leipzig: B. G. Teubner, 1995. Reprinted with the kind permission of K. G. Saur Verlag, München.*

Library of Congress Cataloging-in-Publication Data
Horace.
 [Epistulae. English]
 The epistles of Horace / [translated by] David Ferry.— 1st ed.
   p. cm.
 ISBN 0-374-14856-2 (hardcover : alk. paper)
   1. Rome—Politics and government—Poetry.   2. Epistolary poetry, Latin—
 Translations into English.   3. Political poetry, Latin—Translations into English.
 I. Ferry, David.   II. Title.

PA6396.E5 F45 2001
871'.01—dc21

                                                            00-052746

Designed by Abby Kagan

Frontispiece art: Roman. Paintings. 1st C., 10–1 B.C.
Black Room (Room 15), North Wall: Central pavilion with landscape vignette.
Fresco, black ground. H. 95; W. 48 in. From Villa of Agrippa, Boscotrecase, near
Pompeii. The Metropolitan Museum of Art, Rogers Fund, 1920. (20.192.1)

For my students

and for Sebastian Carrico Wood

CONTENTS

BOOK TWO

INTRODUCTION

Horace (Quintus Horatius Flaccus) was born in Apulia, in the heel of the boot of Italy, in 65 B.C.E. His father was a well-to-do freedman who saw to it that his gifted son received a good education, in Rome and then in Athens. While in Athens Horace joined the army of Brutus, two years after the assassination of Julius Caesar. He became a staff officer and fought, by his own account not very valiantly (Ode ii.7), at the battle of Philippi, where Octavian (later to be the Emperor Augustus) and Mark Antony defeated Brutus. Apparently, as a result, the property of Horace's family was confiscated. But Horace went to Rome and secured a position in the Treasury and, after some time, under the sponsorship of the poet Virgil, was received into the literary circle around Octavian and his chief adviser, Maecenas. Maecenas, especially, became a close friend as well as Horace's patron. It was he who gave Horace his villa, the "Sabine farm," in the countryside a few miles from Rome, near Tibur (now called Tivoli).

In general the story of Horace's quiet life is the story of his writing. First there were the Satires, published in two books (late 30s B.C.E.), the first poems by which he received some recognition. In 29 he published his Epodes, in 23 the first three books of the Odes, and in 20 the first book of his Epistles. Three years later he had the great honor of being asked by Augustus to write a ceremonial poem to be read at the Saecular Games Augustus organized to celebrate his own long reign. Three years after that he published his second book of Epistles, and a year later the fourth book of his Odes. It is not clear when the Epistle to the Pisos ("The Art of Poetry") was written.

Horace died in November, 8 B.C.E., shortly after the death of Maecenas (as he predicted in Ode ii.17).

There's a passage in "The Art of Poetry" that seems to leap out of its immediate context to tell us something essential about Horace's ambition for his art, and it seems specially applicable to the art of these verse letters:

My aim is to take familiar things and make
Poetry of them, and do it in such a way
That it looks as if it was easy as could be
For anybody to do it (although he'd sweat
And strain and work his head off, all in vain).
Such is the power of judgment, of knowing what
It means to put the elements together
In just the right way; such is the power of making
A perfectly wonderful thing out of nothing much.

This joyfulness about skill and performance is what we experience over and over again when we read the Epistles. We are witnesses to the exhilarated pleasure of the artist in what he has made and, indeed, what he is making before our eyes and as we are listening. Not only in the poems about poetry among these Epistles but everywhere else in them, sometimes implicitly, sometimes not, the experience of the writer as he is writing is manifest, and our pleasure as we share in that of the poems may be Horace's principal motive for writing them.

It's the voice that's the life of these poems: so free, so confident, so knowledgeable about himself, and about work, so contemptuous of pretense, so entertaining, so joyful. The voice is an invention, of course, or a playing field of inventions, but it gives the illusion of speaking to us as we hear it with a startlingly familiar immediacy. In the Epistles, Horace perfected the hexameter verse medium in which his voice performs, always as if conversationally, speaking in these letters with such directness, wit, and urgency, to young writers, to friends, to his patron, to the Emperor Augustus himself. It is the voice of a free man talking about how to get along in a Roman world full of temptations, opportunities, and contingencies, and how to do so with your integrity intact. And Rome comes alive in the voice:

festinat calidus mulis gerulisque redemptor,
torquet nunc lapidem, nunc ingens machina tignum,
tristia robustis luctantur funera plaustris,
hac rabiosa fugit canis, hac lutulenta ruit sus:
i nunc et versus tecum meditare canoros!

Oh, sure. Tell me about it. First there'll be
A contractor with his gear and all his workmen,
And then a giant crane in the way, first hoisting
A great huge stone and then a great huge log,

And then here comes a funeral procession
Jostling its way along through all the traffic
Of great huge rattling wagons, and all of a sudden
A mad dog runs by one way through the street
And a filthy runaway pig the other way.
"Work on writing sonorous verses enroute?"
(ii.2)

Or:

Si fortunatum species et gratia praestat,
mercemur servum qui dictet nomina, laevum
qui fodicet latus et cogat trans pondera dextram
porrigere: 'hic multum in Fabia vale, ille Velina . . .'

If being in favor with power is what you value,
Purchase a slave to murmur a name in your ear
And give you a nudge in the ribs so you know it's time
To stretch your glad hand out across the street—
"That man over there has got a lot of say
With the Fabian tribe; that other's got a lot
Among the Velini . . ."
(i.6)

It's a voice that's on a civilizing mission, fully aware of all its difficulties, of how the temptations and contingencies are always there, in such a world and in our own natures:

fervet avaritia miseroque cupidine pectus?
sunt verba et voces quibus hunc lenire dolorem
possis et magnam morbi deponere partem.
laudis amore tumes? sunt certa piacula quae te
ter pure lecto poterunt recreare libello.
invidus, iracundus, iners, vinosus, amator
nemo adeo ferus est ut non mitescere possit,
si modo culturae patientem commodet aurem.

. . . Are you burning up
With avarice? There are spells and sayings to use

To make the fever abate, and make you better.
All swollen up with love of glory, are you?
There are charms you can use to bring the swelling down,
If you read the book three times and faithfully follow
The rites prescribed especially for your trouble.
Nobody's so far gone in savagery —
A slave of envy, wrath, lust, drunkenness, sloth —
That he can't be civilized, if he'll only listen
Patiently to the doctor's good advice.
(i.1)

Or:

cervus equum pugna melior communibus herbis
pellebat, donec minor in certamine longo
imploravit opes hominis frenumque recepit;
sed postquam victor violens discessit ab hoste,
non equitem dorso, non frenum depulit ore . . .

The stag was a better fighter than the horse
And often drove him out of their common pasture,
Until the horse, the loser, asked man's help
And acquiesced in taking the bit in his mouth.
But after his famous victory in this battle
He couldn't get the rider off his back
And he couldn't get the bit out of his mouth.
(i.10)

Or:

nos numerus sumus et fruges consumere nati,
sponsi Penelopae nebulones Alcinoique
in cute curanda plus aequo operata iuventus,
cui pulchrum fuit in medios dormire dies et
ad strepitum citharae cessantem ducere somnum.

Ut iugulent hominem, surgunt de nocte latrones:
ut te ipsum serves, non expergisceris? atqui
si noles sanus, curres hydropicus . . .

We're nothing but ciphers, born only to eat and drink,
Penelope's no-account suitors, or we're like those
Young men at Alcinous' court, who are so busy
Primping and grooming and sleeking their precious complexions,
Sleeping till noon, and to the sound of the cithara
Whiling the night away till sleepy time comes.
Cutthroats get up at night to cut men's throats.
Surely you could get up to save yourself.
Better take care of yourself while you're still well,
Or you're going to have to do it when you get sick.
(i.2)

Toward the end of the Epistle to Augustus Horace says:

Rather than poetry of the sort I write
That keeps itself so close to the level ground,
I'd much prefer to be able to be the teller
Of tales of heroic deeds, of barbarous kingdoms,
Far-off lands and rivers, forts built high
In mountain fastnesses, the Parthians
Transfixed by the power of dread of Caesar's might,
And all wars finally brought to an end, so that
The Gate of guardian Janus can be closed.
I wish I had the power to do what I wish.
But the grandeur of your deeds is out of scale
For such poetry as mine; and my self-knowledge
Keeps me from trying for more than I have the strength for.
(ii.1)

There are disingenuous playfulness and very large claims in the modesty of this. The grandeur of Augustus's deeds is out of scale for such poetry as his, though not, the context says, out of scale for Virgil or Varius; but in fact the list of things Horace says he can't do is a list of what he himself had recently and brilliantly done, or was doing at about this same time, in the celebratory Odes 3, 4, 14, and 15 of Book Four. But the largest claim is in *sermones . . . repentis per humum*, poetry "that keeps itself so close to the level ground," and in *nec meus audet / rem temptare pudor quam vires ferre recusent* ("and my self-knowledge / Keeps me from trying for more than I have the strength for"). The central values of Horace's life and his poetry, and the sources of the freedom of his voice, are implicit in the standards of self-knowledge and the respect for limitations that this passage only *seems* to apologize for. It is the level ground he has staked out as his territory, and he has done so with the exultation of a conqueror, making something beautiful out of nothing much. Awareness of one's self and of the actual unheroic everyday world one lives in and deals with is the condition of that heroic freedom it is the business of these poems, in all their variety, to celebrate.

Over and over again the poems celebrate the freedom that is synonymous with this awareness and with the maintaining of one's integrity:

> *Qui melior servo, qui liberior sit avarus,*
> *in triviis fixum cum se demittit ob assem,*
> *non video. nam qui cupiet, metuet quoque; porro,*
> *qui metuens vivet, liber mihi non erit umquam.*

> *I find it hard to say how the greedy man*
> *Is less a slave than the slave, when, slave to his nature,*
> *He stoops and tries and tries to pinch a penny*
> *Loose from the pavement some kid has soldered it to.*
> *Anxiety owns the man who is owned by greed;*
> *He whom anxiety owns is therefore a slave.*
> *(i.16)*

And:

> *certum voto pete finem.*
> *invidus alterius macrescit rebus opimis;*
> *invidia Siculi non invenere tyranni*
> *maius tormentum.*

> *Set limits to what your desires make you long for;*
> *When his neighbor grows fat the covetous man grows thin.*
> *The worst Sicilian tyrant couldn't invent*
> *A torment worse than envy.*
> *(i.2)*

And:

> *utque sacerdotis fugitivus liba recuso,*
> *pane egeo iam mellitis potiore placentis.*

I'm like that slave who ran away because
They fed him honey cakes and he longed for bread.
(i.10)

And (to his patron Maecenas):

nec somnum plebis laudo satur altilium nec
otia divitiis Arabum liberrima muto;
saepe verecundum laudasti rexque paterque
audisti coram, nec verbo parcius absens:
inspice si possum donata reponere laetus.
Haud male Telemachus, proles patientis Ulixei:
'non est aptus equis Ithace locus . . .'

I don't go in for praising the poor man's lot
Just as I've finished off an excellent dinner,
But I wouldn't trade my independence, either,
For all the gold Arabia could offer.
You've praised me often enough for moderation,
And to your face I've called you "king" and "father,"
And I'd use such words about you behind your back.
But see if I wouldn't cheerfully return
All of the gifts you generously have given.
Ulysses' son Telemachus got it right,
When he said to Menelaus when Menelaus
Had offered him a gift of chariot horses,
"Thanks, but Ithaca isn't right for horses . . ."
(i.7)

And the poems that are more particularly about poetry exultantly promulgate the same values as the poems that are (*sed verae numerosque modosque ediscere vitae*) about "the cadences and meter of living right." In "The Art of Poetry" Horace says:

In the days when men still wandered in the woods,
Orpheus, holy interpreter of the gods,
Taught us to shun the life of blood and killing.
Therefore there's the story of how his music
Tamed the ravening beasts, the lions and tigers;

And there's the story too of how the trance
Of Amphion playing his enchanting music
Caused the stones to move and rise and go
To do his bidding, building the walls of Thebes.
This was the wisdom of song in days gone by:
To know how to tell the difference between
Public and private, the sacred and the profane;
To curb licentiousness and put in place
The rules of marriage; establish cities and
On wooden tablets write down settled laws.
Thus honor and glory as to divinities came
To the earliest poets and to the songs they sang.
(ii.3)

This noble panegyric of the civilizing mission of poetry is characteristic. Still more characteristic of these Epistles is such a passage as this:

People who write bad poetry are a joke,
But writing makes them happy and it makes them
Happily reverential of themselves.
If they hear no praise from you, what do they care?
Deaf to your silence they'll praise themselves, serenely.
But he who desires to write a legitimate poem
Will be an honest critic of what he does.
He won't be afraid, if some expression doesn't
Seem right, if it lacks the appropriate weight or luster,
Or if it's wrong for the tone of the passage it's part of,
To take it away, although it's reluctant to go
And struggles to keep the place it felt enshrined in.
He'll dig up obscure old words such as Cato used,
Or Cethegus used, and bring them back, from where
They'd languished in the dark of the long ago,
Into the light of day, alive with meaning.
He'll be willing to use new words in poetry,
Made valid by their valid use by men
Going about their daily work or play.
Steady, flowing, pure, just as a river
Is steady, flowing, and pure, he will pour forth

Power, and bless his country with a rich language.
He'll prune back whatever is overgrown, smooth out
Whatever is rough, get rid of whatever weakness
Inhibits power; he'll make it look like child's play,
Although, in fact, he tortures himself to do so.
(ii.2)

The play of voice and personality is able to register the downright, flat-out, delighted contemptuousness of *Ridentur mala qui componunt carmina* ("People who write bad poetry are a joke") and the declarative forthrightness of *cum tabulis animum censoris sumet honesti* ("Will be an honest critic of what he does") and to rise from that, by means of figures of speech that characterize the good writer as daringly lawless, lawlessly daring, iconoclast, ransacker of shrines, deposer of false gods (*audebit, quaecumque parum splendoris habebunt / et sine pondere erunt et honore indigna fruentur, / verba movere loco, quamvis invita recedant / et versentur adhuc intra penetralia Vestae*); as a grave robber in his zeal to get rid of the false images, or an Orpheus in his zeal to find and make new that which is old, a hero daring to go to the underworld on a rescue mission (*obscurata diu populo bonus eruet atque / proferet in lucem speciosa vocabula rerum, / quae priscis memorata Catonibus atque Cethegis / nunc situs informis premit et deserta vetustas*). These are comic and heroic figures of speech, and the Latin enjoys its performance in creating them. And enjoyment isn't the only thing about it. It's also the sincerity and nobility of *vehemens et liquidus puroque simillimus amni / fundet opes Latiumque beabit divite lingua* ("Steady, flowing, pure, just as a river / Is steady, flowing, and pure, he will pour forth / Power, and bless his country with a rich language") and then returning from this height, in his characteristic way, to the actualities, the level ground, of the job of work of writing, *luxuriantia compescet, nimis aspera sano / levabit cultu, virtute carentia tollet. / ludentis speciem dabit et torquebitur* ("He'll prune back whatever is overgrown, smooth out / Whatever is rough, get rid of whatever weakness / Inhibits power; he'll make it look like child's play, / Although, in fact, he tortures himself to do so").

In the Epistles the play of Horace's voice exemplifies the values that it also celebrates.

NOTE ON THE TRANSLATION

In translating the Epistles I have used iambic pentameter, with frequent anapestic substitutions, as my metrical system. In English a six-foot line comparable to Horace's hexameters would, in my opinion, be impossible to manage without extreme artificiality. I have, however, in a few instances, concluded a poem with a six-foot rather than a five-foot line, and in my translation of Epistle ii.3 ("The Art of Poetry") there are a few places where I've departed from the pentameter in order to allude to, though not to reproduce, other meters Horace is discussing.

Let me echo a statement I made in my translation of Horace's Odes: In these translations I have tried, generally speaking, to be as faithful as I could be to Horace's poems. English of course is not Latin and I am most certainly not Horace. Every act of translation is an act of interpretation, and every choice of English word or phrase, every placement of those words or phrases in sentences—made in obedience to the laws and habits of English, not Latin, grammar, syntax, and idioms—and every metrical decision—made in obedience to English, not Latin, metrical laws and habits—reinforces the differences between the interpretation and the original. This is true however earnestly the interpretation aims to represent the sense of Horace's Epistles, the effects and implications of his figures of speech, the controlled volatility of his tones of voice. As translations of these Epistles go, it is my hope that this one, granting such differences between English and Latin, is reasonably close.

BOOK ONE

Prima dicte mihi, summa dicende Camena,
spectatum satis et donatum iam rude quaeris,
Maecenas, iterum antiquo me includere ludo?
non eadem est aetas, non mens. Veianius armis
Herculis ad postem fixis latet abditus agro,
ne populum extrema rediens exoret harena.
est mihi purgatam crebro qui personet aurem:
'solve senescentem mature sanus equum, ne
peccet ad extremum ridendus et ilia ducat.'
nunc itaque et versus et cetera ludicra pono:
quid verum atque decens curo et rogo et omnis in hoc sum.
condo et compono quae mox depromere possim.
ac ne forte roges quo me duce, quo Lare tuter,
nullius addictus iurare in verba magistri,
quo me cumque rapit tempestas, deferor hospes.
nunc agilis fio et mersor civilibus undis
virtutis verae custos rigidusque satelles;
nunc in Aristippi furtim praecepta relabor
et mihi res, non me rebus, subiungere conor.

i.1

TO MAECENAS

Maecenas, you were the first to be named in the first
Poem I ever wrote and you'll be the first
To be named in the last I'm ever going to write,
So why on earth, Maecenas, do you persist
In trying to send a beat-up old-timer like me
Back into the ring? I'm not what I used to be,
Not in age and not in inclination.
Veianius, you know, the famous gladiator,
Has hung up his arms at the door of Hercules
And gone to hide away someplace in the country.
He doesn't want to have to keep on asking
Over and over for favor from the crowd.
I'm getting used to hearing people say,
"A word to the wise: send the old horse out to pasture
Before he falls down while everybody jeers,"
And so I'm giving up my verses and all
Other foolishness of the sort, and now
Devote myself entirely to the study
Of what is genuine and right for me,
Storing up what I learn for the sake of the future.
You ask me where my home and shelter is,
Who's my protector now? No one at all.
I'm bound by oath to no one but myself.
Wherever I happen to be when a storm comes up,
I make for the nearest port, whatever it is.
One moment you see me busy doing good,
Active in all the causes, champion of virtue,
And then the next I furtively slip back into
The study of Aristippus's rules on how

Ut nox longa quibus mentitur amica diesque
longa videtur opus debentibus, ut piger annus
pupillis quos dura premit custodia matrum,
sic mihi tarda fluunt ingrataque tempora, quae spem
consiliumque morantur agendi naviter id quod
aeque pauperibus prodest, locupletibus aeque,
aeque neglectum pueris senibusque nocebit.
restat ut his ego me ipse regam solerque elementis.
non possis oculo quantum contendere Lynceus,
non tamen idcirco contemnas lippus inungi;
nec, quia desperes invicti membra Glyconis,
nodosa corpus nolis prohibere cheragra.
est quadam prodire tenus, si non datur ultra.
fervet avaritia miseroque cupidine pectus?
sunt verba et voces quibus hunc lenire dolorem
possis et magnam morbi deponere partem.
laudis amore tumes? sunt certa piacula quae te
ter pure lecto poterunt recreare libello.
invidus, iracundus, iners, vinosus, amator
nemo adeo ferus est ut non mitescere possit,
si modo culturae patientem commodet aurem.

Virtus est vitium fugere et sapientia prima
stultitia caruisse. vides, quae maxima credis
esse mala, exiguum censum turpemque repulsam,

To make the world serve me, not me the world.
Just as the night seems to go on forever
For the lover whose mistress has deserted him,
Just as the day seems never to end for one
Who has to labor all day long for his bread,
Just as the year seems endless for the youth
Who's not yet free of his mother's household rule,
Just so, the hours drag on that hinder me
In my ambition to advance myself
In the sort of project that, if carried out
Successfully, is good for anyone,
Whether rich or poor, and its failure is bound to be
Harmful to anyone, whether he's young or old.

I have to do my best with what I've got.
Suppose you don't have eyes as good as Lynceus;
That doesn't mean that if they're sore you wouldn't
Use salve to make them better; suppose you haven't
A chance in the world of competing with undefeated
Glycon the strongman, that doesn't mean you wouldn't
Try everything you could by exercise
To keep away rheumatic aches and pains.
You can't do everything, but you have to do
Everything you can. Are you burning up
With avarice? There are spells and sayings to use
To make the fever abate, and make you better.
All swollen up with love of glory, are you?
There are charms you can use to bring the swelling down,
If you read the book three times and faithfully follow
The rites prescribed especially for your trouble.
Nobody's so far gone in savagery—
A slave of envy, wrath, lust, drunkenness, sloth—
That he can't be civilized, if he'll only listen
Patiently to the doctor's good advice.

Virtue begins by shunning vice; wisdom
By shunning folly. Look at the trouble and risk
You're willing to take to avoid what you think are the worst

quanto devites animi capitisque labore.
impiger extremos curris mercator ad Indos,
per mare pauperiem fugiens, per saxa, per ignis:
ne cures ea quae stulte miraris et optas,
discere et audire et meliori credere non vis?
quis circum pagos et circum compita pugnax
magna coronari contemnat Olympia, cui spes,
cui sit condicio dulcis sine pulvere palmae?
vilius argentum est auro, virtutibus aurum.

'O cives, cives, quaerenda pecunia primum est,
virtus post nummos.' haec Ianus summus ab imo
prodocet, haec recinunt iuvenes dictata senesque.
laevo suspensi loculos tabulamque lacerto
est animus tibi, sunt mores, est lingua fidesque,
sed quadringentis sex septem milia desunt:
plebs eris. at pueri ludentes 'rex eris' aiunt,
'si recte facies.' hic murus aeneus esto,
nil conscire sibi, nulla pallescere culpa.
Roscia, dic sodes, melior lex an puerorum est
nenia, quae regnum recte facientibus offert,
et maribus Curiis et decantata Camillis?
isne tibi melius suadet qui rem facias, rem,
si possis, recte, si non, quocumque modo, rem,
ut propius spectes lacrimosa poemata Pupi,
an qui Fortunae te responsare superbae
liberum et erectum praesens hortatur et aptat?

Things of all that could possibly happen: defeat
At the polls, perhaps, or maybe the loss of a fortune.
You are, for example, a merchant eager for gain,
So off you go as far as the farthest Indies,
And all to get away from poverty,
No matter at what risk of storms at sea,
Of shipboard fires, or hidden rocks or shoals.
Why don't you listen and learn from someone who knows
Better than you how to quit competing for
And caring about what you care about and compete for
So foolishly?

         Listen to someone like me—
(What fighter in the dusty arena wouldn't
As soon be crowned with the wreath without the dust?)
Gold is worth more than silver, virtue's worth more
Than gold. Here is the way the moneymen talk,
Down by the Arch of Janus: "Citizens, listen,
Get money first, get virtue after that."
That's what you hear wherever you go these days.
"Suppose you have good sense, and eloquence,
You have good morals, your word can always be trusted.
So what? If, nevertheless, you're short of the money
It takes to buy a knighthood, you're just a pleb."
But children at their play have a song that goes:
"He who does right will be a king, all right."
Let this be our defense: not to have any
Wrongdoing on our conscience to worry over.
So tell me, which is better, the things they say
Down by the Arch of Janus, or what the children
Sing and chant as they play their game in the street:
"He who does right will be a king, all right,"
The song that manly Camillus probably sang,
And manly Curius too, when they were kids?
Is it better advice you get from the one who says:
"Fair means or foul, get money if you can;
No matter how you get it, be sure you get it"—
All for a seat down front at some bad play?

Quod si me populus Romanus forte roget cur
non ut porticibus sic iudiciis fruar isdem,
nec sequar aut fugiam quae diligit ipse vel odit,
olim quod vulpes aegroto cauta leoni
respondit referam: 'quia me vestigia terrent
omnia te adversum spectantia, nulla retrorsum.'
belua multorum es capitum. nam quis sequar aut quem?
pars hominum gestit conducere publica; sunt qui
frustis et pomis viduas venentur avaras
excipiantque senes quos in vivaria mittant;
multis occulto crescit res faenore. verum
esto aliis alios rebus studiisque teneri:
idem eadem possunt horam durare probantes?
'nullus in orbe sinus Bais praelucet amoenis,'
si dixit dives, lacus et mare sentit amorem
festinantis eri; cui si vitiosa libido
fecerit auspicium, cras ferramenta Teanum
tolletis, fabri. lectus genialis in aula est?
nil ait esse prius, melius nil caelibe vita:
si non est, iurat bene solis esse maritis.
quo teneam vultus mutantem Protea nodo?
quid pauper? ride: mutat cenacula, lectos,
balnea, tonsores; conducto navigio aeque
nauseat ac locuples, quem ducit priva triremis.

Or better to listen to him whose advice prepares you
To stand up, a free man, defying arrogant Fortune?

What if the Roman people should ask me why,
Since I walk the same streets and under the same
Colonnades as they do, I'm not a lover
Of what they love, or hater of what they hate.
I'd give the answer the fox gave to the lion:
"I see those footprints. I see that those footprints all
Go into your den, and none come out again.
You're a monster with many heads, so why on earth
Do you think I'd be willing to go along with you?"

Who is it I'm supposed to emulate?
Those whose money grows by who knows what?
Those who get their profit from public money?
Those who hunt down widows with charming gifts
Or hornswoggle foolish old men into their nets,
Bringing them in like animals into game parks?

Different people go in for different things,
For this, for that, or the other; that doesn't mean
They won't change their minds an hour later and
Go in for that, this, anything else instead.
"No place more beautiful than Baiae Bay."
The minute the rich man says it, that minute you know
His pleasure in Baiae Bay has spent itself,
And you know his libido will take him another way:
"Workmen, build me a house inland at Teanum."
Is the bed of the household Genius set up in the hall
Of the married man's house? Why of course he says:
"I long for a bachelor life, the best of all."
But move it out of the hall, and then he says,
"Being married, after all, is best of all."
How do you keep the face of this Proteus
From changing, time and time again? The poor man?
Just like the rich man, on a different budget.
As soon as he's in one garret he wants another;

Si curatus inaequali tonsore capillos
occurri, rides; si forte subucula pexae
trita subest tunicae vel si toga dissidet impar,
rides: quid mea cum pugnat sententia secum,
quod petiit spernit, repetit quod nuper omisit,
aestuat et vitae disconvenit ordine toto,
diruit aedificat, mutat quadrata rotundis?
insanire putas sollemnia me neque rides,
nec medici credis nec curatoris egere
a praetore dati, rerum tutela mearum
cum sis et prave sectum stomacheris ob unguem
de te pendentis, te respicientis amici.

Ad summam, sapiens uno minor est Iove, dives,
liber, honoratus, pulcher, rex denique regum,
praecipue sanus—nisi cum pituita molesta est.

He goes to a different public bath every day;
One haircut and he wants to change his barber;
He rents a little boat and gets just as seasick
As the rich man gets on his opulent private yacht.

Maecenas, you notice and laugh if the barber gives me
A crooked haircut or if my worn-out shirt
Shows under the new tunic I just bought
Or if my toga doesn't hang down straight.
But when I don't know what my own mind is,
Hating the thing I just now loved, and wanting
The thing I just rejected scornfully,
Judgment seething and boiling, the order of things
All out of order, pulled down, built up again,
Pulled down, built up, round turned to square, and square
To round again, you're perfectly unperturbed
And not the least disposed to laugh at me,
Nor do you think I need a doctor's help
Or a keeper assigned by the court to take care of me.

The wise man's second only to Jupiter:
He is a king of kings in his own life,
As the Stoics say; free, beautiful, most honored,
And above all else he's reasonable and sane,
Unless, of course, he's got a bad toothache.

Troiani belli scriptorem, Maxime Lolli,
dum tu declamas Romae, Praeneste relegi;
qui quid sit pulchrum, quid turpe, quid utile, quid non,
planius ac melius Chrysippo et Crantore dicit.
cur ita crediderim, nisi quid te detinet, audi.

Fabula, qua Paridis propter narratur amorem
Graecia barbariae lento collisa duello,
stultorum regum et populorum continet aestus.
Antenor censet belli praecidere causam.
quid Paris? ut salvus regnet vivatque beatus
cogi posse negat. Nestor componere litis
inter Peliden festinat et inter Atriden;
hunc amor, ira quidem communiter urit utrumque.
quidquid delirant reges, plectuntur Achivi.
seditione, dolis, scelere atque libidine et ira
Iliacos intra muros peccatur et extra.
rursus quid virtus et quid sapientia possit,
utile proposuit nobis exemplar Ulixen,
qui domitor Troiae multorum providus urbis
et mores hominum inspexit latumque per aequor,
dum sibi, dum sociis reditum parat, aspera multa
pertulit, adversis rerum immersabilis undis.

TO LOLLIUS MAXIMUS

While you're in Rome, studying declamation,
Here I am in Praeneste, reading Homer,
From whom we learn more than we learn from Crantor
Or Chrysippus, and learn it more clearly, about
The good and bad of things, what's helpful to know,
What isn't. I'll tell you why I think so, if
You've got the time and willingness to listen.

The story of how Paris's love affair
Was the cause of the long slow agonizing war
Between the Greeks and that barbarian country
Teaches us what the consequences are
Of the passions of foolish kings and their foolish people.
Antenor had it in mind to eradicate
The cause of the war. And Paris? He absolutely
Refused to take up the option of living in peace
And happily ever after. Nestor was anxious
To settle once and for all the trouble between
Peleus's son and Atreus's son. But love
Inflamed the one, and fury inflamed them both.
People are punished for whatever maddens their kings.
Faction, and intrigue, lust, sacrilege, rage,
Inside or outside Troy it all goes wrong.

And Homer gives an example of what it is
That virtue and wisdom are capable of, by telling
The story of wise Ulysses, tamer of Troy,
Who witnessed the ways of men in many places,
As with his comrades he strove to make his way

Sirenum voces et Circae pocula nosti;
quae si cum sociis stultus cupidusque bibisset,
sub domina meretrice fuisset turpis et excors,
vixisset canis immundus vel amica luto sus.
nos numerus sumus et fruges consumere nati,
sponsi Penelopae nebulones Alcinoique
in cute curanda plus aequo operata iuventus,
cui pulchrum fuit in medios dormire dies et
ad strepitum citharae cessantem ducere somnum.

Ut iugulent hominem, surgunt de nocte latrones:
ut te ipsum serves, non expergisceris? atqui
si noles sanus, curres hydropicus; et ni
posces ante diem librum cum lumine, si non
intendes animum studiis et rebus honestis,
invidia vel amore vigil torquebere. nam cur
quae laedunt oculum festinas demere, si quid
est animum, differs curandi tempus in annum?
dimidium facti, qui coepit, habet: sapere aude:
incipe. qui recte vivendi prorogat horam,
rusticus expectat dum defluat amnis: at ille
labitur et labetur in omne volubilis aevum.
quaeritur argentum puerisque beata creandis
uxor et incultae pacantur vomere silvae:
quod satis est cui contingit, nihil amplius optet.
non domus et fundus, non aeris acervus et auri
aegroto domini deduxit corpore febris,
non animo curas. valeat possessor oportet,
si comportatis rebus bene cogitat uti.

Over the seas to Ithaca and home.
He suffered many adversities, and yet
He never sank beneath the waves of dangers.
You know about the singing of the Sirens,
And Circe's cup. If he had foolishly
And greedily like his fellows drunk from the cup
He would have been changed from what he was into
The loathsome stupid creature of a whore,
Like a filthy dog or a pig in love with muck.

We're nothing but ciphers, born only to eat and drink,
Penelope's no-account suitors, or we're like those
Young men at Alcinous' court, who are so busy
Primping and grooming and sleeking their precious complexions,
Sleeping till noon, and to the sound of the cithara
Whiling the night away till sleepy time comes.
Cutthroats get up at night to cut men's throats.
Surely you could get up to save yourself.
Better take care of yourself while you're still well,
Or you're going to have to do it when you get sick;
If you don't stay up at night with a book and a lamp,
Studying hard to discipline your mind,
You'll toss and turn all night, tormented by
The envy and passion you don't know how to govern.
If you had a sty, you'd be in a hurry to cure it;
If the sickness is in your soul, why put it off?
Get yourself going and you'll be halfway there;
Dare to be wise; get started. The man who puts off
The time to start living right is like the hayseed
Who wants to cross the river and so he sits there
Waiting for the river to run out of water,
And the river flows by, and it flows on by, forever.

Men cultivate the wilderness with a plow,
And hope for money, and a wife to bear their children.
The man who has enough should be satisfied
With what he has. Property is never
Going to be able to cure a body that's sick

qui cupit aut metuit, iuvat illum sic domus et res
ut lippum pictae tabulae, fulmenta podagrum,
auriculas citharae collecta sorde dolentis.
sincerum est nisi vas, quodcumque infundis acescit.

Sperne voluptates: nocet empta dolore voluptas.
semper avarus eget: certum voto pete finem.
invidus alterius macrescit rebus opimis;
invidia Siculi non invenere tyranni
maius tormentum. qui non moderabitur irae,
infectum volet esse dolor quod suaserit et mens,
dum poenas odio per vim festinat inulto.
ira furor brevis est. animum rege, qui nisi paret,
imperat; hunc frenis, hunc tu compesce catena.

Fingit equum tenera docilem cervice magister
ire viam qua monstret eques; venaticus, ex quo
tempore cervinam pellem latravit in aula,
militat in silvis catulus. nunc abbibe puro
pectore vera, puer, nunc te melioribus offer.
quo semel est imbuta recens servabit odorem
testa diu. quod si cessas aut strenuus anteis,
nec tardum opperior nec praecedentibus insto.

Or a mind that's sick. You've got to be well if you want
To enjoy the things you own. If your life is governed
By cravings for what you lack, or else by fear
Of losing what you have, then what you have,
Your house and your possessions, give you as much
Pleasure as a picture gives a blind man,
Or an elegant pair of shoes gives a man with gout,
Or music gives to an ear stuffed up with wax.
A glass that isn't clean will guarantee
That whatever you pour into it will sour.

Take a long, cold, intelligent look at pleasure:
It hurts you if you purchase it with pain;
The avaricious man always feels poor;
Set limits to what your desires make you long for;
When his neighbor grows fat the covetous man grows thin.
The worst Sicilian tyrant couldn't invent
A torment worse than envy. The man whose anger
Gets out of hand will wish he hadn't done
The things he did while raging to satisfy
The hunger of his rage. A fit of rage
Is a fit of genuine honest-to-goodness madness.
Keep control of your passions. If you don't,
Your passions are sure to get control of you.
Keep control of them, bridle them, keep them in chains.
While the horse is still young and while its tender neck
Responds to its trainer's will, it learns how to go
The way its rider wants it to. The hound
Began to learn how to be of use in the woods
The day when it was a pup and barked at the sight
And smell of the skin of a deer hung up in the yard.

Drink in with an open heart what I have to say;
Accept what someone older and wiser offers.
A clean new vessel retains for a very long time
The fragrance of what was first poured into it.
However, if you loiter behind, don't think
I'll wait around for you or, if you rush
Impetuously ahead, come chasing after.

Iuli Flore, quibus terrarum militet oris
Claudius Augusti privignus, scire laboro.
Thraecane vos Hebrusque nivali compede vinctus
an freta vicinas inter currentia turris
an pingues Asiae campi collesque morantur?
quid studiosa cohors operum struit? hoc quoque curo.
quis sibi res gestas Augusti scribere sumit,
bella quis et paces longum diffundit in aevum?
quid Titius, Romana brevi venturus in ora,
Pindarici fontis qui non expalluit haustus,
fastidire lacus et rivos ausus apertos?
ut valet? ut meminit nostri? fidibusne Latinis
Thebanos aptare modos studet auspice Musa
an tragica desaevit et ampullatur in arte?
quid mihi Celsus agit, monitus multumque monendus
privatas ut quaerat opes et tangere vitet
scripta Palatinus quaecumque recepit Apollo,
ne, si forte suas repetitum venerit olim
grex avium plumas, moveat cornicula risum
furtivis nudata coloribus? ipse quid audes?
quae circumvolitas agilis thyma? non tibi parvum
ingenium, non incultum est et turpiter hirtum.

i.3

TO JULIUS FLORUS

I wonder, Florus, where in the world you are?
Where has Tiberius' mission taken you?
Are you in Thrace, by icebound Hebrus, or
By the Hellespont that runs between the towers?
Or somewhere in Asia's fertile fields and hills?
What are your friends, the smart young writers, up to?
Which one is assuming the task of describing the deeds,
Peaceful or warlike, done in Augustus's name?
Who'll be the chronicler, for the sake of the future?
What about Titius? He'll soon be the talk of the town
Because he didn't turn pale at the notion of drawing
From Pindar's well instead of the common cisterns.
Does he ever think about me? How is he doing?
Does he continue to study, watched by the Muses,
Adapting the measures of Thebes to the Latin lyre?
Or does he rant and rage in the tragic mode?
And Celsus, too? He's been advised, and surely
It's good advice for him, that he should write
Out of himself and out of what he knows
And stay away from those old writers he reads
In Apollo's library on the Palatine.
Someday the flock of birds might come back asking
To have their brilliant feathers given back
And the crow, stripped naked, is certain to be laughed at.

And what about you? What are you working on?
What fields of thyme are you hovering over, these days?
You have real gifts; your land is carefully tended,
Not left uncultivated and overgrown.

seu linguam causis acuis seu civica iura
respondere paras seu condis amabile carmen,
prima feres hederae victricis praemia. quod si
frigida curarum fomenta relinquere posses,
quo te caelestis sapientia duceret, ires.
hoc opus, hoc studium parvi properemus et ampli,
si patriae volumus, si nobis vivere cari.

Debes hoc etiam rescribere, si tibi curae
quantae conveniat Munatius; an male sarta
gratia nequiquam coit et rescinditur ac vos
seu calidus sanguis seu veri inscitia vexat
indomita cervice feros? ubicumque locorum
vivitis, indigni fraternum rumpere foedus,
pascitur in vestrum reditum votiva iuvenca.

You'd win the prize, incisively pleading a case,
Or defining the issues of some point of law,
Or writing attractive verses, and you'd deserve it;
And if you're able to learn to do without
Anxiety's chilling effect, you'll be able to follow
The lead of wisdom up to the highest reaches.
Such is the study that each of us ought to pursue,
No matter who we are, if we want to be
Of value to ourselves and to our country.

Tell me, when you answer this letter, whether
You care for Munatius as you ought to do?
Or was the wound of friendship badly stitched up,
And has it torn open again? No matter if
It's inexperience, hot blood, or both, that causes
The trouble between you two unbroken wild horses,
Wherever on earth you are—you two who ought
To know better than to break the fraternal bond—
A votive calf is waiting for your return.

Albi, nostrorum sermonum candide iudex,
quid nunc te dicam facere in regione Pedana?
scribere quod Cassi Parmensis opuscula vincat
an tacitum silvas inter reptare salubris
curantem quidquid dignum sapiente bonoque est?

Non tu corpus eras sine pectore. di tibi formam,
di tibi divitias dederunt artemque fruendi.
quid voveat dulci nutricula maius alumno
qui sapere et fari possit quae sentiat et cui
gratia, fama, valetudo contigat abunde
et mundus victus non deficiente crumina?

Inter spem curamque, timores inter et iras,
omnem crede diem tibi diluxisse supremum.
grata superveniet quae non sperabitur hora.
me pinguem et nitidum bene curata cute vises,
cum ridere voles, Epicuri de grege porcum.

i.4

TO THE POET TIBULLUS

Albius, honest reader of my poems,
What shall I say you're doing, out there in the country?
At work on a poem to outdo Cassius?
Taking a calm salubrious walk in the woods,
And thinking thoughts that are worthy of yourself?

You never were a body without a soul.
The gods gave you good looks and they gave you money,
And gave you the art of being pleased with their gifts.
What more could a governess want for the sweet child she raises,
Than that he should know and that he be able to say
What's honest and right, and that he should act upon it,
And that he be granted favor and fame and good health,
And the money to live an agreeable kind of life?

Between hope and discouragement, fears, and angers, and such,
Treat every new day as the last you're going to have,
Then welcome the next as unexpectedly granted.

When you want a good laugh you'll find me here, in the pink,
A pig from Epicurus's sty, fat, sleek, well cared for.

Si potes Archiacis conviva recumbere lectis
nec modica cenare times holus omne patella,
supremo te sole domi, Torquate, manebo.
vina bibes iterum Tauro diffusa palustris
inter Minturnas Sinuessanumque Petrinum.
si melius quid habes, arcesse, vel imperium fer.
iamdudum splendet focus et tibi munda supellex.
mitte levis spes et certamina divitiarum
et Moschi causam. cras nato Caesare festus
dat veniam somnumque dies; impune licebit
aestivam sermone benigno tendere noctem.

Quo mihi fortunam, si non conceditur uti?
parcus ob heredis curam nimiumque severus
assidet insano. potare et spargere flores
incipiam patiarque vel inconsultus haberi.
quid non Ebrietas dissignat? operta recludit,
spes iubet esse ratas, ad proelia trudit inertem,
sollicitis animis onus eximit, addocet artis.
fecundi calices quem non fecere disertum,
contracta quem non in paupertate solutum?

i.5

TO TORQUATUS

If it doesn't bother you much to recline on modest
Benches of the sort that Archias makes,
And if a simple dinner on unpretentious
Dishes doesn't alarm you, then, Torquatus,
I'll expect you just at sundown at my house.
You'll have wine that comes from the region between Petrinum
And marshy Minturnae, dating from the time
Of the second consulship of Statilius Taurus.
If you have better, send it along, or else
Be pleased with what I have. All is prepared;
The furniture's set out; the hearth is swept.
So put aside ambition and striving for money,
And put aside for a while the cause of Moschus.
Tomorrow's Caesar's birthday; we can sleep late;
We can talk the night away agreeably.

What's money for, if it isn't put to use?
It's crazy to scrimp and save, all for the sake
Of leaving it to some heir to use it up.
So let the drinking start and the flowers be scattered.
Tell me I'm a spendthrift, if you want to,
But look what drinking can do! It reveals what's hidden;
It tells you that you'll get what you always wanted;
It pushes the coward right out into the battle;
It lifts the anxious burden from troubled hearts;
It helps you do what you couldn't do before.
Who hasn't been made more eloquent by drink?
However confined in poverty, tell me, who hasn't
Been freed for a while from feeling that he's unfree?

Haec ego procurare et idoneus imperor et non
invitus, ne turpe toral, ne sordida mappa
corruget naris, ne non et cantharus et lanx
ostendat tibi te, ne fidos inter amicos
sit qui dicta foras eliminet, ut coeat par
iungaturque pari. Butram tibi Septiciumque
et nisi cena prior potiorque puella Sabinum
detinet assumam. locus est et pluribus umbris;
sed nimis arta premunt olidae convivia caprae.
tu quotus esse velis rescribe et rebus omissis
atria servantem postico falle clientem.

Here's what I willingly promise to offer tonight:
No dirty napkins to turn your nose up at;
The couch covers neat as can be, without a wrinkle;
Your cup and your dish shined up as to be your mirror;
Nobody there to tell on you what you said;
Congenial people meeting congenial people.
Butra and Septicus, both, will be invited,
And Sabinus, unless he has a better offer,
A better dinner and a good-looking girl.
There will be room at the table for "the shades,"
The extra uninvited, but not too many.
Too many people, the room would be like a stable.

Write me a note and tell me who to invite;
Then hurry on down; put a sign on your office door
And leave by the back, so none of your clients will see you.

Nil admirari prope res est una, Numici,
solaque quae possit facere et servare beatum.
hunc solem et stellas et decedentia certis
tempora momentis sunt qui formidine nulla
imbuti spectent: quid censes munera terrae,
quid maris extremos Arabas ditantis et Indos,
ludicra quid, plausus et amici dona Quiritis,
quo spectanda modo, quo sensu credis et ore?
qui timet his adversa, fere miratur eodem
quo cupiens pacto; pavor est utrubique molestus,
improvisa simul species exsternat utrumque.
gaudeat an doleat, cupiat metuatne, quid ad rem,
si, quidquid vidit melius peiusve sua spe,
defixis oculis animoque et corpore torpet?
insani sapiens nomen ferat, aequus iniqui,
ultra quam satis est virtutem si petat ipsam.

I nunc, argentum et marmor vetus aeraque et artis
suspice, cum gemmis Tyrios mirare colores;
gaude quod spectant oculi te mille loquentem.

i.6

TO NUMICIUS

The way to be happy and stay so, Numicius, is:
Never to be bowled over. Some men can gaze
Unstupefied by the sight of the sun and the stars
As they move around in their courses in the sky.
But what about you? What happens to you when you think
Of the fabulous gifts that earth and sea yield up,
The riches of far-off India and Arabia,
The spectacles and shows, the favor, the applause
Of the Roman crowd? How is it that *you're* affected?
The man who's ruled by the horrified vision of how
Such things can be lost and vanish is overawed
In just the same way as the man who's ruled by the thrill
Of their very existence. Both are made dizzy
By the vivid prospect of what they fear or long for.
Elation, trepidation, it's all the same,
If when a man sees something turn out to be
Much better or worse than he thought it was going to be,
He gazes in wonder at it, transfixed, struck dumb.
Call even the wise man mad, the just unjust,
Who goes overboard, even to follow virtue.

Survey with admiring pride those precious things,
The bronzes, antique marbles, silver, all
Your works of art, the Tyrian cloths, the jewels.
Feel the exhilaration when the crowd
Gathers in numbers just to hear *you* speak;
Be early down at the Forum, late to get home,
So Mutus, who comes from lesser stock than you,
Won't make more money than you, and therefore you

quidquid sub terra est in apricum proferet aetas;
defodiet condetque nitentia. cum bene notum
porticus Agrippae, via te conspexerit Appi,
ire tamen restat Numa quo devenit et Ancus.

Si latus aut renes morbo temptantur acuto,
quaere fugam morbi. vis recte vivere, quis non?
si virtus hoc una potest dare, fortis omissis
hoc age deliciis. virtutem verba putas et
lucum ligna? cave ne portus occupet alter,
ne Cibyratica, ne Bithyna negotia perdas;
mille talenta rotundentur, totidem altera. porro et
tertia succedant et quae pars quadret acervum.
scilicet uxorem cum dote fidemque et amicos
et genus et formam regina Pecunia donat
ac bene nummatum decorat Suadela Venusque.
mancipiis locuples eget aeris Cappadocum rex:
ne fueris hic tu. chlamydes Lucullus, ut aiunt,
si posset centum scaenae praebere rogatus
'qui possum tot?' ait: 'tamen et quaeram et quot habebo
mittam.' post paulo scribit sibi milia quinque
esse domi chlamydum; partem vel tolleret omnis.
exilis domus est ubi non et multa supersunt
et dominum fallunt et prosunt furibus. ergo,

Won't have to be lost in admiration of him.
Time will bring to light whatever lies hidden
Beneath the earth; whatever there is that shines
So brightly now will be buried someday in the dark.
After you've been the cynosure of all eyes
On the Appian Way or near Agrippa's columns
You still have to go where Numa went, and Ancus.

When you have a pain in your belly or in your side,
You work on getting rid of it, don't you? Therefore,
If you want to live right (and who doesn't?) and if
You agree that the only way to do it is
To learn to be good, then patiently settle down
To the work of getting rid of the faults you have.
But if you think that goodness is nothing more
Than a matter of words, no more than that, and if
When you look at a forest, all you see is the wood,
Be very careful lest a competitor
Make it to port before you, taking away
The custom you had hoped for for your lumber.

Suppose you've rounded off a stack of talents,
Exactly a thousand, then a second stack,
Exactly a thousand also, stack up a third,
And then a fourth—why not?—to make a square.
Of course the goddess Money brings gifts with her:
A wealthy wife, and friends, position, looks,
High social standing, everything, the lot;
And the goddesses Venus and Influence, too, adorn
The man who has it all. Don't be like that king
In Cappadocia who had a lot of slaves
But didn't have much money. Lucullus, when asked,
So the story goes, if he had a hundred cloaks
To be used in some theater piece or other, replied,
"I can't think I have *that* many, but let me go look."
After a while he returned and said, "Well, it seems
I have five thousand cloaks; go help yourself."
That house is poor indeed that doesn't have

si res sola potest facere et servare beatum,
hoc primus repetas opus, hoc postremus omittas.
navus mane Forum et vespertinus pete tectum,
ne plus frumenti dotalibus emetat agris
Mutus et (indignum, qui sit peioribus ortus)
hic tibi sit potius quam tu mirabilis illi.

Si fortunatum species et gratia praestat,
mercemur servum qui dictet nomina, laevum
qui fodicet latus et cogat trans pondera dextram
porrigere: 'hic multum in Fabia valet, ille Velina;
cui libet hic fascis dabit eripietque curule
cui volet importunus ebur.' 'frater,' 'pater' adde;
ut cuique est aetas, ita quemque facetus adopta.

Si bene qui cenat bene vivit, lucet, eamus
quo ducit gula, piscemur, venemur, ut olim
Gargilius, qui mane plagas, venabula, servos
differtum transire Forum Campumque iubebat,
unus ut e multis populo spectante referret
emptum mulus aprum. crudi tumidique lavemur,
quid deceat, quid non, obliti, Caerite cera
digni, remigium vitiosum Ithacensis Ulixei,
cui potior patria fuit interdicta voluptas.

Si, Mimnermus uti censet, sine amore iocisque
nil est iucundum, vivas in amore iocisque.

Vive, vale. si quid novisti rectius, istis
candidus imperti; si nil, his utere mecum.

Much more than it needs, so the master won't have to notice
How much the servants take away from him.
So if getting rich is the thing that makes you happy,
Then my advice is, by all means, get rich,
Keep at it, incessantly busy, don't ever give up.

If being in favor with power is what you value,
Purchase a slave to murmur a name in your ear
And give you a nudge in the ribs so you know it's time
To stretch your glad hand out across the street—
"That man over there has got a lot of say
With the Fabian tribe; that other's got a lot
Among the Velini; that man coming along
Could give the fasces to anyone he wanted,
And if he wanted to he could pull the bench
Right out from under any judge he chose."
And when you greet whoever the somebody is,
Be sure to call him "Father!" or "Brother!," depending.

If eating well is living well, well then,
Let's go, it's dawn, let appetite be our guide,
Let's fish, let's hunt, the way Gargilius did,
Making his servants set out with all their gear,
Their spears and nets, being sure to be seen
By everyone down in the Forum, and later be seen
Triumphantly making their way back home again,
With, on the back of a mule, a slain wild boar
(One that they'd surreptitiously bought at the market).
Then, straight from the table where we gorged ourselves,
Let's go right off to the Public Baths, who cares,
As heedless of how to behave as the voteless rabble.
If, as Mimnermus says, there's no fun in living
If living's no fun, then let's have fun, why not?

Goodbye, take care. If you know better rules
To be guided by, please tell me what they are.
If you want to follow these, you're welcome to them.

Quinque dies tibi pollicitus me rure futurum
Sextilem totum mendax desideror. atqui,
si me vivere vis sanum recteque valentem,
quam mihi das aegro, dabis aegrotare timenti,
Maecenas, veniam, dum ficus prima calorque
dissignatorem decorat lictoribus atris
dum pueris omnis pater et matercula pallet
officiosaque sedulitas et opella forensis
adducit febris et testamenta resignat.
quod si bruma nives Albanis illinet agris,
ad mare descendet vates tuus et sibi parcet
contractusque leget. te, dulcis amice, reviset
cum Zephyris, si concedes, et hirundine prima.

Non quo more piris vesci Calaber iubet hospes
tu me fecisti locupletem. 'vescere, sodes.'
'iam satis est.' 'at tu quantumvis tolle.' 'benigne.'
'non invisa feres pueris munuscula parvis.'
'tam teneor dono quam si dimittar onustus.'
'ut libet. haec porcis hodie comedenda relinques.'
prodigus et stultus donat quae spernit et odit:
haec seges ingratos tulit et feret omnibus annis.

TO MAECENAS

I know I promised to stay only a week
Down in the country, and now I'm breaking my promise,
I'm staying down here all August. But if you really
Want me to be as fit as a fiddle, why then
You'll treat me the way you would if I were sick,
And not just always afraid of getting sick,
In the season when the heat and unripe figs
Give the undertaker's helpers all dressed in black
A lot to do, and all the mothers and fathers
Are pale and anxious about the health of the kids,
And when the round of official business and
Of social duties in the heat-struck Forum
Brings fever on and causes the opening up
And reading of last wills and testaments.
And when winter brings down snow on the Alban Hills
Your bard is going to take himself to the seashore,
And, snug as a bug in a rug, curl up with a book.
Dear friend, if you'll allow, come Spring's first zephyrs,
He'll visit you with the first returning swallow.

The manner in which you've made me rich is different
From the manner in which some Calabrian host might offer
Pears to his dinner guest: "Please have some pears."
"No, thanks." "Then take some home, take all you want."
"No, thanks." "Your kids will love them, take them, take them."
"No, thanks, but thank you anyway for the thought."
"Oh, well, the pigs will eat what you don't want."
The wastrel gives away what he's fool enough
Not to know the value of; the seed
That's scattered that way has always produced a bumper

vir bonus et sapiens dignis ait esse paratus,
nec tamen ignorat quid distent aera lupinis;
dignum praestabo me etiam pro laude merentis.
quod si me noles usquam discedere, reddes
forte latus, nigros angusta fronte capillos,
reddes dulce loqui, reddes ridere decorum et
inter vina fugam Cinarae maerere protervae.

Forte per angustam tenuis cornicula rimam
repserat in cumeram frumenti pastaque rursus
ire foras pleno tendebat corpore frustra.
cui mustela procul 'si vis' ait 'effugere istinc,
macra cavum repetes artum, quem macra subisti.'
hac ego si compellar imagine, cuncta resigno.
nec somnum plebis laudo satur altilium nec
otia divitiis Arabum liberrima muto;
saepe verecundum laudasti rexque paterque
audisti coram, nec verbo parcius absens:
inspice si possum donata reponere laetus.

Haud male Telemachus, proles patientis Ulixei:
'non est aptus equis Ithace locus, ut neque planis
porrectus spatiis nec multae prodigus herbae.
Atride, magis apta tibi tua dona relinquam.'

Crop of ungratefulness, and it always will.
The wise good man is ready to help the worthy,
But he's always able to tell the difference between
What's real money and what's only stage money.
Certainly I have every intention of being
Deserving of all your kindnesses to me,
But if you want me always to be around,
Then give me back my youth, and a strong body,
A full black head of hair, and ready laughter,
An easy way of talking, and shared amusement,
Over our drinks, as we complain about
Cynara's latest betrayal of a lover.

Once there was a little skinny fox
Who found a chink in the side of a closed-up bin
And crawled in through it to eat the corn inside,
And he ate so much he got too fat to get out.
A weasel witnessed this and said to him:
"If you want to get out again you have to be
Skinny enough to get out as you got in."
I take the point, and if applied to me
I'd give up all the things you've given me.
I don't go in for praising the poor man's lot
Just as I've finished off an excellent dinner,
But I wouldn't trade my independence, either,
For all the gold Arabia could offer.
You've praised me often enough for moderation,
And to your face I've called you "king" and "father,"
And I'd use such words about you behind your back.
But see if I wouldn't cheerfully return
All of the gifts you generously have given.
Ulysses' son Telemachus got it right,
When he said to Menelaus when Menelaus
Had offered him a gift of chariot horses,
"Thanks, but Ithaca isn't right for horses.
There's not a lot of grass to forage on,
And not a lot of level ground, and so,
I'll leave your gifts to you as fit for you."
Modest things are right for modest people;

parvum parva decent. mihi iam non regia Roma,
sed vacuum Tibur placet aut imbelle Tarentum.

Strenuus et fortis causisque Philippus agendis
clarus, ab officiis octavam circiter horam
dum redit atque Foro nimium distare Carinas
iam grandis natu queritur, conspexit, ut aiunt,
arrasum quendam vacua tonsoris in umbra
cultello proprios resecantem leniter unguis.
'Demetri' puer hic non laeve iussa Philippi
accipiebat, 'abi, quaere et refer, unde domo, quis,
cuius fortunae, quo sit patre quove patrono.'
it, redit et narrat, Vulteium nomine Menam,
praeconem, tenui censu, sine crimine, notum
et properare loco et cessare, et quaerere et uti,
gaudentem parvisque sodalibus et Lare certo
et ludis et post decisa negotia Campo.
'scitari libet ex ipso quodcumque refers. dic
ad cenam veniat.' non sane credere Mena,
mirari secum tacitus. quid multa? 'benigne'
respondet. 'neget ille mihi?' 'negat improbus et te
neglegit aut horret.' Vulteium mane Philippus
vilia vendentem tunicato scruta popello
occupat et salvere iubet prior. ille Philippo
excusare laborem et mercennaria vincla
quod non mane domum venisset, denique quod non
providisset eum. 'sic ignovisse putato
me tibi si cenas hodie mecum.' 'ut libet.' 'ergo
post nonam venies. nunc i, rem strenuus auge.'

Rome, queen of cities, isn't what pleases me most,
But quiet Tibur and peaceful Tarentum are.

Philippus, the famous advocate, who was
An energetic, effective, important man,
Was heading home from work one afternoon
And grousing (he wasn't as young as he once had been)
About how far the Carinae, where his home was,
Was from the Forum. He happened to notice a man,
Sitting in the shade of an empty barber's stall,
Paring his nails himself with his own knife.
Philippus said to Demetrius, his slave boy,
"Go find out who that is and where he comes from,
Who's his father, or who's his patron, and what
Does he do for a living." He went, he asked, he came back.
He said the name of the man was Volteius Mena,
A sidewalk vendor, of slender means, with a good record,
A self-sufficient man, a good hard worker
When hard work was required, a good idler
When idling was in order; he made enough
To spend on what he wanted; he had a home,
And a little group of friends he took pleasure in,
And at the end of the working day he enjoyed
The sports at the Circus and at the Campus Martius.
"I'd like him to tell me about himself himself.
Invite him to supper." Volteius was very surprised
And was silent for a while, and finally said,
"No, thank you." "He said no? To me?" "Why, yes."
"The fellow's insolent, or else he's scared."

The next day Philippus happened to see Volteius,
Who was selling trinkets to people on the street,
And Philippus was the first to say hello.
Volteius made excuses for not having come
To Philippus's house to pay his respects and thank him,
And Philippus replied, "Well, I'll forgive you if you
Promise to come to my house for dinner today."
"Thank you, I will." "Good. Come at three-thirty,
And until that time good luck with the things you're selling."

Ut ventum ad cenam est, dicenda tacenda locutus
tandem dormitum dimittitur. hinc ubi saepe
occultum visus decurrere piscis ad hamum,
mane cliens et iam certus conviva iubetur
rura suburbana indictis comes ire Latinis.
impositus mannis arvum caelumque Sabinum
non cessat laudare. videt ridetque Philippus
et, sibi dum requiem, dum risus undique quaerit,
dum septem donat sestertia, mutua septem
promittit, persuadet uti mercetur agellum.
mercatur. ne te longis ambagibus ultra
quam satis est morer, ex nitido fit rusticus atque
sulcos et vineta crepat mera, praeparat ulmos,
immoritur studiis et amore senescit habendi.
verum ubi oves furto, morbo periere capellae,
spem mentita seges, bos est enectus arando,
offensus damnis media de nocte caballum
arripit iratusque Philippi tendit ad aedis.
quem simul aspexit scabrum intonsumque Philippus,
'durus' ait, 'Vultei, nimis attentusque videris
esse mihi.' 'pol, me miserum, patrone, vocares,
si velles' inquit 'verum mihi ponere nomen.
quod te per Genium dextramque deosque Penatis
obsecro et obtestor, vitae me redde priori.'

Qui semel aspexit quantum dimissa petitis
praestent, mature redeat repetatque relicta.
metiri se quemque suo modulo ac pede verum est.

So Volteius went to his house for supper and they
Talked their heads off together on this or that subject
And had a great time. Volteius was hooked like a fish.
Having been patronized, one time, with a dinner,
He very soon became a constant guest,
And when the holidays came Philippus asked him
Down to his place in the country outside Rome.
On the way down there in the carriage he couldn't stop praising
The Sabine countryside and climate. Philippus
Took note of this and smiled and, because he craved
Diversion and amusement wherever he might
Possibly find it, offered Volteius a gift
Of seven thousand sesterces and also a loan
Of seven thousand more, to buy a farm.
So Volteius bought one. To make a long story short,
This self-sufficient city guy was changed
Into an instant rustic and talked of nothing
But furrows and vines and preparing the elms for the vines,
And made himself old and almost died from trying
To learn how to make a success of his Sabine farm.
But after his sheep were stolen and after his goats
Got sick and died, and after his crops all failed,
And his ox fell down exhausted in its traces,
In the middle of the night one night he saddled his horse
And rode in a towering rage to Philippus's house.
When Philippus saw him looking the way he looked,
Filthy and all out of order, he said, "My friend,
It seems to me you look as if you've been
Working too hard, and are under some sort of strain."
"For God's sake, patron," Volteius replied, "if you
Knew what to call me you'd know to call me wretched.
I beg you, in the name of your household gods,
Return me to the life I had before."

It's right that the man who sees how what he spurned
Surpasses what he spurned it for should seek
To get it back. Each man should be able to be
The judge of what's right for himself by his own standards.

Celso gaudere et bene rem gerere Albinovano
Musa rogata refer, comiti scribaeque Neronis.

Si quaeret quid agam, dic multa et pulchra minantem
vivere nec recte nec suaviter; haud quia grando
contuderit vitis oleamve momorderit aestus,
nec quia longinquis armentum aegrotet in agris;
sed quia mente minus validus quam corpore toto
nil audire velim, nil discere quod levet aegrum;
fidis offendar medicis, irascar amicis
cur me funesto properent arcere veterno;
quae nocuere sequar, fugiam quae profore credam,
Romae Tibur amem ventosus, Tibure Romam.

Post haec, ut valeat, quo pacto rem gerat et se,
ut placeat iuveni percontare, utque cohorti.
si dicet 'recte,' primum gaudere, subinde
praeceptum auriculis hoc instillare memento:
'ut tu fortunam, sic nos te, Celse, feremus.'

i.8

TO CELSUS ALBINOVANUS

Muse, take this message, please, to Nero's friend
And secretary, Celsus: "Greetings to you
And all best wishes," signed, "Sincerely, Horace."
If he should ask you how I am, please tell him,
"Not very well." Nothing is going right,
Nothing is pleasant, though everything ought to be.
It's not that hail has flattened my vines or heat
Parched out my olive trees; my cattle haven't
Come down with some sickness they got in the far pastures.
It's that I'm much less well in mind than body;
Unwilling to listen to anything anyone tells me
To make me better. I bark at my faithful physicians;
I'm angry at my friends because they try
To interfere between my torpor and me.
It's that I follow whatever is bad for me
And shun the things that might be good for me.
When I'm in Rome I want to be at Tibur;
When I'm at Tibur I want to be in Rome.

Then ask him how *he* is, how is his work,
Is he in favor still with his patron prince
And with the entourage? And if he answers,
"Oh, very well indeed," congratulate him,
But also be sure to give him this advice:
"We'll put up with you as you with your good luck."

Septimius, Claudi, nimirum intellegit unus
quanti me facias. nam cum rogat et prece cogit
scilicet, ut tibi se laudare et tradere coner,
dignum mente domoque legentis honesta Neronis,
munere cum fungi propioris censet amici,
quid possim videt ac novit me valdius ipso.
multa quidem dixi cur excusatus abirem;
sed timui mea ne finxisse minora putarer,
dissimulator opis propriae, mihi commodus uni.
sic ego, maioris fugiens opprobria culpae,
frontis ad urbanae descendi praemia. quod si
depositum laudas ob amici iussa pudorem,
scribe tui gregis hunc et fortem crede bonumque.

i.9

TO TIBERIUS CLAUDIUS NERO CAESAR

Apparently Septimius knows my standing
Better than I, for when, by asking me,
And really, by force of pleading, forcing me
To recommend him as being worthy of joining
The entourage of Nero, who's known to value
Honesty and virtue above all else,
And when, by thinking, as Septimius seems to,
That I occupy a position closer than his,
He has more knowledge of what I'm capable of
Than I myself have. I gave him lots of reasons
Why I ought to be excused; but I was afraid
That he might think that maybe I was really
Pretending to have *less* influence than I have,
Perhaps to keep my influence for myself.
And so, in order to escape being thought
Guilty of having this more serious fault,
I have to go in for a city forwardness.

But if it turns out that you agree with me
That a friend's entreaty is a kind of command,
You will condone my putting shame aside,
And take my friend Septimius into your household,
Believing me when I say he's brave and good.

Urbis amatorem Fuscum salvere iubemus
ruris amatores. hac in re scilicet una
multum dissimiles, at cetera paene gemelli
fraternis animis, quidquid negat alter, et alter,
annuimus pariter. vetuli notique columbi
tu nidum servas, ego laudo ruris amoeni
rivos et musco circumlita saxa nemusque.
quid quaeris? vivo et regno simul ista reliqui
quae vos ad caelum fertis rumore secundo,
utque sacerdotis fugitivus liba recuso,
pane egeo iam mellitis potiore placentis.
vivere naturae si convenienter oportet
ponendaeque domo quaerenda est area primum,
novistine locum potiorem rure beato?
est ubi plus tepeant hiemes, ubi gratior aura
leniat et rabiem Canis et momenta Leonis,
cum semel accepit solem furibundus acutum?
est ubi divellat somnos minus invida cura?
deterius Libycis olet aut nitet herba lapillis?
purior in vicis aqua tendit rumpere plumbum

i.10

TO ARISTIUS FUSCUS

Dear Fuscus, I, a lover of the country,
Send greetings to you, a lover of the city.
It's true, we differ in this; in everything else
It's just as if we were twins, with brotherly hearts;
One shakes his head, the other one shakes his head;
One nods his head, the other one nods his head;
We're like a pair of good old turtledoves.

But you love the city, so you never leave it;
I love the country, so I go on praising
Brooks and groves and mossy rocks and such.
I feel I'm truly living, truly myself,
The minute I leave the city and everything
You city lovers lavish praises on.
I'm like that slave who ran away because
They fed him honey cakes and he longed for bread.

If we're supposed quote "to live in accordance with
The nature of things" unquote and therefore have to
Choose where best to do so, then, I ask you,
Is any place better for this than the blessèd country?
Where are the winters milder? Tell me, where else
Could you with anything like such pleasure feel
The cooling breeze that calms the rabid Dog Star
And the raging Lion struck by the Sun's fierce arrows?
Is there anywhere else where sleep is so untroubled?
Is the grass less fragrant or less shining than
Libyan mosaics? Is the water that does its best
To burst the leaden pipes in city streets

quam quae per pronum trepidat cum murmure rivum?
nempe inter varias nutritur silva columnas
laudaturque domus longos quae prospicit agros.
Naturam expellas furca, tamen usque recurret
et mala perrumpet furtim fastidia victrix.

Non qui Sidonio contendere callidus ostro
nescit Aquinatem potantia vellera fucum
certius accipiet damnum propiusve medullis
quam qui non poterit vero distinguere falsum.
quem res plus nimio delectavere secundae,
mutatae quatient. si quid mirabere, pones
invitus. fuge magna: licet sub paupere tecto
reges et regum vita praecurrere amicos.
cervus equum pugna melior communibus herbis
pellebat, donec minor in certamine longo
imploravit opes hominis frenumque recepit;
sed postquam victor violens discessit ab hoste,
non equitem dorso, non frenum depulit ore:
sic, qui pauperiem veritus potiore metallis
libertate caret, dominum vehit improbus atque
serviet aeternum, quia parvo nesciet uti.
cui non conveniet sua res, ut calceus olim,
si pede maior erit, subvertet, si minor, uret.
laetus sorte tua vives sapienter, Aristi,
nec me dimittes incastigatum, ubi plura
cogere quam satis est ac non cessare videbor.
imperat aut servit collecta pecunia cuique,
tortum digna sequi potius quam ducere funem.

Haec tibi dictabam post fanum putre Vacunae,
excepto quod non simul esses, cetera laetus.

Purer than water that makes its murmuring way
Downhill in mountain streams? In your atria,
Among your elaborate columns, you've planted trees,
And houses with views of the fields are always praised.
Drive Nature out with a pitchfork, she'll come right back,
Victorious over your ignorant confident scorn.

The man who doesn't know the difference between
Wool dyed with Sidonian purple or just with dyes
From Aquinum isn't as badly off as the man
Who isn't able to tell the true from the false.
Change will upset the man who's always been lucky.
You hate to lose what you've always been pleased to have.
Avoid the grand: you can live in a little house
And still live better than kings and the friends of kings.

The stag was a better fighter than the horse
And often drove him out of their common pasture,
Until the horse, the loser, asked man's help
And acquiesced in taking the bit in his mouth.
But after his famous victory in this battle
He couldn't get the rider off his back
And he couldn't get the bit out of his mouth.
The man who's afraid to be poor and therefore gives
His liberty away, worth more than gold,
Will carry a master on his back and be
A slave forever, not knowing how to live
On just a little. If what he happens to have
Won't fit a man, it's as it is with a shoe:
Too big, it makes you stumble; too small, it pinches.

Aristius, you'll be wise if you live happy
With what you have. And if you see me set
On having more for myself than I ought to have,
Don't let me get away with it unreproved.
The money you have is either your master or slave.
The leash should be held by you, not by your money.

I'm writing out back of Vacuna's ancient shrine,
Happy in every way, except that you're not here.

Quid tibi visa Chios, Bullati, notaque Lesbos,
quid concinna Samos, quid Croesi regia Sardis,
Zmyrna quid et Colophon? maiora minorane fama?
cunctane prae Campo et Tiberino flumine sordent?
an venit in votum Attalicis ex urbibus una?
an Lebedum laudas odio maris atque viarum?
scis Lebedus quid sit? Gabiis desertior atque
Fidenis vicus. tamen illic vivere vellem
oblitusque meorum obliviscendus et illis
Neptunum procul e terra spectare furentem.

Sed neque qui Capua Romam petit imbre lutoque
aspersus volet in caupona vivere nec, qui
frigus collegit, furnos et balnea laudat
ut fortunatam plene praestantia vitam,
nec, si te validus iactaverit Auster in alto,
idcirco navem trans Aegaeum mare vendas.
incolumi Rhodos et Mytilene pulchra facit quod
paenula solstitio, campestre nivalibus auris,
per brumam Tiberis, Sextili mense caminus.

i.11

TO BULLATIUS

So, Bullatius, what did you think of Chios?
What did you think of famous Lesbos? Or Smyrna?
Or Croesus's royal Sardis, or Colophon?
Or elegant Samos? Tell me, no matter whether
They're more or less than what you had expected,
Is any one of these places anything other
Than disappointing compared to the Campus Martius
Or to the Tiber? Or is it your heart's desire
To see at least one of the Atallids' cities, or, tired
Of seasides and highways, is Lebedus what you're after?
You know what it's really like there—not even Fidena's,
Not even Gabii's, more desolate and deserted.

"Nevertheless, I long to be there alone,
Forgetting the world, and glad to be forgotten,
Gazing from afar at Neptune's violence."

But a man who has traveled from Capua to Rome
And arrives at an inn all muddy and wet and chilled,
Wouldn't want to live on forever at the inn,
No matter how cozy he's made by its stove and hot baths.
If you arrived on the other side of the sea,
Safe and sound, after a stormy crossing,
You wouldn't therefore decide to sell the ship
On which you were going to get back home again.
To a sensible free man, being away in Rhodes
Or beautiful Mitylene is like wearing
A heavy overcoat in the summertime,
Or wearing a loincloth in the wintertime

dum licet et vultum servat Fortuna benignum,
Romae laudetur Samos et Chios et Rhodos absens.

Tu, quamcumque deus tibi fortunaverit horam,
grata sume manu neu dulcia differ in annum,
ut, quocumque loco fueris, vixisse libenter
te dicas; nam si ratio et prudentia curas,
non locus effusi late maris arbiter, aufert,
caelum, non animum, mutant qui trans mare currunt.
strenua nos exercet inertia; navibus atque
quadrigis petimus bene vivere. quod petis hic est,
est Ulubris, animus si te non deficit aequus.

To go in swimming in the freezing Tiber;
It's lighting up a stove in the middle of August.
While Fortune smiles on you and you're able to,
Stay home in Rome, while praising Samos and Chios
And Rhodes, and so on, as long as they're far away.

Whatever good things the god sees fit to give you,
Take them with thanks; don't think you can save them up
For a rainy day. You want to be able to say
You've lived a happy life. It's reason, good sense,
That takes away your cares; it isn't owning
A house at the shore that has a commanding view.
He only changes his scene, he doesn't change
His mind, who rushes to go abroad. How many
Are busy going elsewhere getting nowhere;
But if you have a healthy attitude,
Then what you're seeking to find can always be found
Right where you are, even in froggy Ulúbrae.

Fructibus Agrippae Siculis quos colligis, Icci,
si recte frueris, non est ut copia maior
ab Iove donari possit tibi. tolle querelas;
pauper enim non est cui rerum suppetit usus.
si ventri bene, si lateri est pedibusque tuis, nil
divitiae poterunt regales addere maius.
si forte in medio positorum abstemius herbis
vivis et urtica, sic vives protinus, ut te
confestim liquidus Fortunae rivus inauret,
vel quia naturam mutare pecunia nescit
vel quia cuncta putas una virtute minora.
miramur si Democriti pecus edit agellos
cultaque, dum peregre est animus sine corpore velox,
cum tu inter scabiem tantam et contagia lucri
nil parvum sapias et adhuc sublimia cures:
quae mare compescant causae, quid temperet annum,
stellae sponte sua iussaene vagentur et errent,
quid premat obscurum, lunae quid proferat orbem,
quid velit et possit rerum concordia discors,
Empedocles an Stertinium deliret acumen?
verum seu piscis seu porrum et caepe trucidas,

TO ICCIUS

Iccius, if you're getting as much enjoyment
As you ought to be getting, out there in Sicily,
Being in charge of Agrippa's rich country estates,
You couldn't ask more from Jupiter himself.
No one is poor who can use whatever he has.

But if you're the kind who prefers to live on nettles
No matter what abundance is all around you,
No doubt you'd go on just the same as if
Fortune had poured an avalanche of gold
Down on your head. Either your nature is such
That money has no effect on it whatsoever,
Or else you value virtue exclusively.
We're amazed at the story of Democritus and how
His cattle ate up his crops while his mind wandered off,
Wherever it wanted, free of the body's confinement.
You too, though exposed to the itch and temptation of riches,
Seem nevertheless to care only for thinking high thoughts:
"What governs the tides? What governs the turning year?
Whether the stars wander about the sky
As they themselves choose or whether some law
Is telling them how to behave? Where did the moon go?
What hid it away in the dark? What brought it back,
Shining again in the sky? What does it mean
To say all things are explained by *concordia discors*?
Is Empedocles crazy, or is it Stertinius?"

Be all that as it may, and whether it's fish,
Or onions and leeks, you slaughter for your menu,

utere Pompeio Grospho et, si quid petet, ultro
defer; nil Grosphus nisi verum orabit et aequum.
vilis amicorum est annona, bonis ubi quid deest.

Ne tamen ignores quo sit Romana loco res,
Cantaber Agrippae, Claudi virtute Neronis
Armenius cecidit; ius imperiumque Phraates
Caesaris accepit genibus minor; aurea fruges
Italiae pleno defudit Copia cornu.

Be nice to Pompeius Grosphus and treat him well.
He'll never make unreasonable requests.
Friends offer easy terms when people need them.

Just so you'll know how things are going in Rome:
Agrippa's valor has brought the Cantabrians down,
And Claudius Nero the Armenians, too,
Phraates kneeling accepts the rule of Caesar.
The golden horn pours out its plenty upon us.

Ut proficiscentem docui te saepe diuque,
Augusto reddes signata volumina, Vinni,
si validus, si laetus erit, si denique poscet.
ne studio nostri pecces odiumque libellis
sedulus importes opera vehemente minister.
si te forte meae gravis uret sarcina chartae,
abicito potius quam quo perferre iuberis
clitellas ferus impingas Asinaeque paternum
cognomen vertas in risum et fabula fias.
viribus uteris per clivos, flumina, lamas.
victor propositi simul ac perveneris illuc,
sic positum servabis onus, ne forte sub ala
fasciculum portes librorum, ut rusticus agnum,
ut vinosa glomus furtivae Pirria lanae,
ut cum pilleolo soleas conviva tribulis.

i.13

TO VINIUS ASINA

Just as I've told you over and over, Vinny,
Deliver these books of mine to Augustus only
If you know for sure that he's in good health and only
If you know for sure that he's in a good mood and only
If it comes about that he asks in person to see it.
I'm worried you'll be so eager to help me you'll botch it,
And I'll be a figure of fun because of you.
If the bagful of books annoys you by being too heavy,
Throw it away, anything rather than bring it
Into his presence and plop it resentfully down,
Turning your patronymic, Asina, into
A joke that everyone there has a good laugh at.

Struggle manfully on, making your way
Over mountains and rivers and swamps, through snow and sleet;
Be careful about how you carry it, not, for example,
Under your armpit, the way some hayseed carries
A lamb to market, or as a drunken housemaid
Tries to conceal a ball of wool she stole,
Or a poor man invited to dinner by some rich cousin
Carries his felt hat and sandals, not knowing what else
To do. And Vinny, please, when you finally get there,
Don't tell whoever you meet what it cost you in sweat
To carry this bag of poems all the way there,

neu vulgo narres te sudavisse ferendo
carmina quae possint oculos aurisque morari
Caesaris; oratus multa prece nitere porro.

Vade, vale, cave ne titubes mandataque frangas.

These poems of mine that might just possibly catch
The attention of Caesar's eyes and Caesar's ears.

Go on, keep on, no matter who tries to stop you,
Go on, farewell, be careful, Vinny, watch out,
Through heat and cold and dark of night, don't stumble.
Handle with care this precious package of mine.

Vilice silvarum et mihi me reddentis agelli,
quem tu fastidis habitatum quinque focis et
quinque bonos solitum Variam dimittere patres,
certemus, spinas animone ego fortius an tu
evellas agro et melior sit Horatius an res.

Me quamvis Lamiae pietas et cura moratur
fratrem maerentis, rapto de fratre dolentis
insolabiliter, tamen istuc mens animusque
fert et avet spatiis obstantia rumpere claustra.
rure ego viventem, tu dicis in urbe beatum:
cui placet alterius, sua nimirum est odio sors.
stultus uterque locum immeritum causatur inique:
in culpa est animus, qui se non effugit umquam.

Tu mediastinus tacita prece rura petebas;
nunc urbem et ludos et balnea vilicus optas:
me constare mihi scis et discedere tristem,
quandocumque trahunt invisa negotia Romam.

i.14

TO THE MANAGER OF HIS FARM

Manager of my woods and my little estate,
Which restores me to myself and which you scorn,
Although it supports five families and sends
Five worthy heads of household to Vicovaro,
Let's vie with one another to see who's better,
You at clearing brambles from the land,
Or me at clearing brambles from the mind.
Let's see which one of the two is in better shape,
Whether it's Horace himself or his Sabine farm.

Although I have to linger here in Rome
Because of my dear Lamia's care and sorrow,
Grieving as he is for his brother's death,
I long with all my heart and mind to break
Through the constraints that hold me back from returning.
I call that man blessed who lives in the country;
And *you* call blessed the one who lives in town.
Naturally someone who envies the situation
Of someone else is going to hate his own.
Each of the two is foolish to blame the place.
It doesn't deserve it; the trouble is in the mind,
Which cannot ever get away from itself.

When you were slaving in Rome at dreary work,
You longed to be down in the country, and now you're there,
Steward of my estate, you long for the city,
The baths, the games, and all that; and as for me,
As you well know, I'm always the same about this:
I'm always sad when I have to set off to do
Some hateful business or other in the city.

non eadem miramur; eo disconvenit inter
meque et te. nam quae deserta et inhospita tesqua
credis, amoena vocat mecum qui sentit et odit
quae tu pulchra putas. fornix tibi et uncta popina
incutiunt urbis desiderium, video, et quod
angulus iste feret piper et tus ocius uva,
nec vicina subest vinum praebere taberna
quae possit tibi nec meretrix tibicina, cuius
ad strepitum salias terrae gravis. et tamen urges
iampridem non tacta ligonibus arva bovemque
disiunctum curas et strictis frondibus exples;
addit opus pigro rivus, si decidit imber,
multa mole docendus aprico parcere prato.

Nunc, age, quid nostrum concentum dividat audi.
quem tenues decuere togae nitidique capilli,
quem scis immunem Cinarae placuisse rapaci,
quem bibulum liquidi media de luce Falerni,
cena brevis iuvat et prope rivum somnus in herba.
nec lusisse pudet, sed non incidere lusum.
non istic obliquo oculo mea commoda quisquam
limat, non odio obscuro morsuque venenat.
rident vicini glaebas et saxa moventem.
cum servis urbana diaria rodere mavis.

We just don't like the same things. What you think of
As dreary inhospitable wilderness,
People like me call lovely, and we all hate
The things that you consider beautiful.
It's the brothels, I see, and the smoky little cafés
That arouse your desire to be in the city, not here
Where the earth yields nothing better than some meager
Pepper and spice, no wine, and where there's no tavern
For you to have a drink in, and no whore
Playing the flute for you to cavort to the tune of.
What's more, you have to sweat and strain to plow
The field no hoe has touched for years, and then
Unyoke the ox and fill him up with the fodder
You had to strip the leaves for, and after that,
When you're worn out, maybe it's rained, and so
You have to build up dams to keep the brook
From running over into the nearby meadow.

Here's what keeps us from singing the same tune:
He who once looked good, with his shining hair
And his spiffy city clothes, and who, although
He hadn't a sou, still somehow managed to please
His avaricious Cynara, and enjoyed
His cup of the best Falernum at lunch each day,
Is now content to have the simplest meal
And then a nap on the grass beside the brook.
It's not the folly of foolishness that's shameful;
The shame is not knowing when folly's time is over.

Down here in the country nobody's sidelong look
Takes away from my simple pleasures or poisons them
With the subtle indirections of city malice.
My country neighbors laugh out loud when they see me
Moving sods and stones this way and that.
You'd love to be eating in town with the city slaves;
You'd love to be in with them, part of the scene.
My city groom would love to be here in the country;

horum tu in numerum voto ruis: invidet usum
lignorum et pecoris tibi calo argutus et horti.
optat ephippia bos, piger optat arare caballus.
quam scit uterque, libens censebo exerceat artem.

He covets your flock, your firewood, and your garden.
The ox wishes he wore the horse's saddle;
The horse, tired of riders, longs for the plow.
Let man and beast be content with what they're best at.

Quae sit hiems Veliae, quod caelum, Vala, Salerni,
quorum hominum regio et qualis via (nam mihi Baias
Musa supervacuas Antonius, et tamen illis
me facit invisum, gelida cum perluor unda
per medium frigus; sane murteta relinqui
dictaque cessantem nervis elidere morbum
sulpura contemni vicus gemit, invidus aegris
qui caput et stomachum supponere fontibus audent
Clusinis Gabiosque petunt et frigida rura.
mutandus locus est et deversoria nota
praeteragendus equus. 'quo tendis? non mihi Cumas
est iter aut Baias' laeva stomachosus habena
dicet eques; sed equi frenato est auris in ore),
maior utrum populum frumenti copia pascat,
collectosne bibant imbris puteosne perennis
iugis aquae (nam vina nihil moror illius orae.
rure meo possum quidvis perferre patique;

i.15

TO NUMONIUS VALA

Vala, what's the winter like at Velia?
Tell me about the climate at Salerno.
What are the people like? Are there good roads?
Musa, my doctor, has seen to it that Baiae's
Absolutely out of the question for me,
And furthermore he's seen to it that I'm
Extremely unpopular there, now that he makes me
Pour ice water over myself in the middle of winter.
Naturally Baiae grumbles because its groves
Of myrtle are now no longer what one resorts to,
And its sulfur hot baths scorned, so celebrated
Once upon a time for being good
For everything that ails one, and they're miffed
By invalids who go away to put
Their heads and shoulders under Clusium's waters
Or else to plunge in Gabii's frigid baths.
So I have to change my route and drive right past
The old familiar places. "Where are you going?
This isn't the way to Baiae or to Cumae"—
That's what the rider will angrily say to his horse,
But the horse has the bit in his mouth and won't be turned.

Tell me, what town down there is the best for food?
Do they have fresh water there, flowing from springs
The whole year round, or do they have to use
Rainwater collected in tanks and saved for the purpose?
No point in even asking about the wine.
At home I'm used to putting up with whatever;
But when I go away I want to have

ad mare cum veni, generosum et lene requiro,
quod curas abigat, quod cum spe divite manet
in venas animumque meum, quod verba ministret,
quod me Lucanae iuvenem commendet amicae),
tractus uter pluris lepores, uter educat apros,
utra magis piscis et echinos aequora celent,
pinguis ut inde domum possim Phaeaxque reverti,
scribere te nobis, tibi nos accredere par est.

Maenius, ut rebus maternis atque paternis
fortiter absumptis urbanus coepit haberi,
scurra vagus, non qui certum praesepe teneret,
impransus non qui civem dinosceret hoste,
quaelibet in quemvis opprobria fingere saevus,
pernicies et tempestas barathrumque macelli,
quidquid quaesierat ventri donabat avaro.
hic ubi nequitiae fautoribus et timidis nil
aut paulum abstulerat, patinas cenabat omasi
vilis et agninae, tribus ursis quod satis esset;
scilicet ut ventres lamna candente nepotum
diceret urendos, correctus Bestius. idem
quidquid erat nactus praedae maioris, ubi omne
verterat in fumum et cinerem, 'non hercule miror'
aiebat 'si qui comedunt bona, cum sit obeso
nil melius turdo, nil vulva pulchrius ampla.'
nimirum hic ego sum. nam tuta et parvula laudo
cum res deficiunt, satis inter vilia fortis;
verum ubi quid melius contingit et unctius, idem
vos sapere et solos aio bene vivere, quorum
conspicitur nitidis fundata pecunia villis.

Something a whole lot nicer, smooth and mellow,
Infusing hopefulness into the heart and veins,
Good for banishing care and promoting a flow
Of eloquence to make some lady think
That I'm still young when it's perfectly clear I'm not.
Which town down there is better for serving rabbit,
Which for wild boar, which one is better for fish,
So I'll come back home as fat as a Phaeacian?
Write me a letter; you're my authority.

Maenius with great spirit squandered all
The inheritance he had from his father and mother,
And so became an extra man and sponge,
A parasite with no fixed place of his own,
Who when he needed a dinner would gladly dine out
On vicious scandal he spread with impartial justice
About both friend and foe. And when he wasn't
Able to wangle an invitation he lived
On dishes of cheap gray lamb, inveighing against
Gluttons and prodigals, saying they ought to be branded.
But when he ate well he ate it all up and said,
"My heavens, this ragout of quail is simply delicious."

I'm just like that. When there isn't a lot to be had,
I'm very good at praising moderation;
But when there's something better and richer offered,
Why then I'm very good at praising how
You rich men live it up in your splendid houses.

Ne perconteris fundus meus, optime Quinti,
arvo pascat erum an bacis opulentet olivae,
pomisne an pratis an amicta vitibus ulmo,
scribetur tibi forma loquaciter et situs agri.

Continui montes, ni dissocientur opaca
valle, sed ut veniens dextrum latus aspiciat sol,
laevum decedens curru fugiente vaporet.
temperiem laudes. quid si rubicunda benigni
corna vepres et pruna ferant? si quercus et ilex
multa fruge pecus, multa dominum iuvet umbra?
dicas adductum propius frondere Tarentum.
fons etiam rivo dare nomen idoneus, ut nec
frigidior Thracam nec purior ambiat Hebrus,
infirmo capiti fluit utilis, utilis alvo.
hae latebrae dulces, etiam, si credis, amoenae,
incolumem tibi me praestant Septembribus horis.

Tu recte vivis si curas esse quod audis.
iactamus iampridem omnis te Roma beatum;
sed vereor ne cui de te plus quam tibi credas,
neve putes alium sapiente bonoque beatum,

TO QUINCTIUS

I'll answer your questions about my place in the country
Before you even ask them, Quinctius, whether
It's crops produced in the fields, or olive trees,
Or apple trees, or pastures, or maybe elms
Supporting grapevines, or whatever, that I get rich from.
I'll ramble on and tell you what it's like.

There are hills all round, surrounding a valley that's shady
Except that in the morning there's the light
Of the rising sun, and the warmth of the setting sun
As he departs in his chariot in the evening.
You'd like the climate and approve of it.
If I were to tell how the shrubs and little trees
Yield ruddy berries and plums and all such things
And the oak and ilex make the cattle happy
With what falls from the boughs, and make their herdsman
Happy because of the cooling shade, you'd say
Tarentum in all its verdure had been brought here.
Then there's the brook, that's almost a little river,
As cool and pure as Hebrus flowing through Thrace.
Its waters are good for everything that ails one.
This refuge, believe me, keeps me safe and sound
Here in retreat from the heat of late summer days.
And *you* live rightly, if you truly live
As you are said to live by all of us
Who have for so long talked of you as happy.
But there's always the fear that one might put more credence
In what other people have to say than in
One's own considered judgment of one's self,

neu, si te populus sanum recteque valentem
dictitet, occultam febrem sub tempus edendi
dissimules, donec manibus tremor incidat unctis.
stultorum incurata pudor malus ulcera celat.
si quis bella tibi terra pugnata marique
dicat et his verbis vacuas permulceat auris,
'tene magis salvum populus velit an populum tu,
servet in ambiguo qui consulit et tibi et urbi
Iuppiter,' Augusti laudes agnoscere possis:
cum pateris sapiens emendatusque vocari,
respondesne tuo, dic, sodes, nomine? 'nempe
vir bonus et prudens dici delector ego ac tu.'
qui dedit hoc hodie cras, si volet auferet, ut, si
detulerit fascis indigno, detrahet idem.
'pone, meum est' inquit: pono tristisque recedo.
idem si clamet furem, neget esse pudicum,
contendat laqueo collum pressisse paternum,
mordear opprobriis falsis mutemque colores?
falsus honor iuvat et mendax infamia terret
quem nisi mendosum et medicandum?

                              Vir bonus est quis?
'qui consulta patrum, qui leges iuraque servat,
quo multae magnaeque secantur iudice lites,
quo res sponsore et quo causae teste tenentur.'

Or that perhaps one might think happiness
Derives from something other than wisdom and virtue,
Or that though everybody says one's fit
And healthy as can be, one might disguise
The secret illness one might have, until
The trembling of one's hands at dinner betrays it.
They're fools who hide the sickness because of shame.

Suppose somebody praised your service in wars
On land or sea, and stroked your listening ears
With words like these: "Let Jupiter be the judge,
Which of these loves was the greater of the two,
The love of the people for him or his for the people,"
You'd certainly be flattered, and certainly like it,
But still you'd know that language like this was fitter
For Caesar Augustus than it was for you.
When you let somebody speak of you as perfect,
A paragon of wisdom and of virtue,
Tell me, do you own up, full of yourself,
"Why yes, that's me. How nice of you to say so."
But those who say such things today are free
To say quite different things about you tomorrow.
If they give the badge of office to me and I'm
Unworthy of it, then they can take it away.
"Take off that badge right now," they'd say, and so
 might be a little sad, but I'd have to comply.
If the very same people should say that I'm a thief,
An utterly shameless villain, capable of
Strangling my poor old father with a rope,
Am I supposed to turn pale and be all upset?
There's something wrong with you if you're exalted
Up to the skies by praise you don't deserve
Or utterly cast down by the opposite,
Which you also don't deserve.

                    Who *is* the good man?
It's the man who knows the laws and strictly obeys them
And is himself a person whose judgment counts

sed videt hunc omnis domus et vicinia tota
introrsum turpem, speciosum pelle decora.
'nec furtum feci nec fugi' si mihi dicit
servus, 'habes pretium: loris non ureris' aio.
'non hominem occidi.' 'non pasces in cruce corvos.'
'sum bonus et frugi.' renuit negitatque Sabellus.
cautus enim metuit foveam lupus accipiterque
suspectos laqueos et opertum miluus hamum.
oderunt peccare boni virtutis amore:
tu nihil admittes in te formidine poenae;
sit spes fallendi, miscebis sacra profanis.
nam de mille fabae modiis cum surripis unum,
damnum est, non facinus, mihi pacto lenius isto.
vir bonus, omne Forum quem spectat et omne tribunal,
quandocumque deos vel porco vel bove placat,
'Iane pater!' clare, clare cum dixit 'Apollo!'
labra movet metuens audiri: 'pulchra Laverna,
da mihi fallere, da iusto sanctoque videri,
noctem peccatis et fraudibus obice nubem.'

Qui melior servo, qui liberior sit avarus,

In matters of property and business and
Whose testimony in a court of law
Can often determine the way a case will go."
And yet his family and his household and
His neighbors, those who really know him, know
That under the plausible decorous outside hide
There hides the corrupt inside. What if a slave
Said this to me: "I've never stolen a thing;
I've never run away." I answer him, "O.K.
Your prize for this is that you've never been beaten."
"I've never killed a man!" "So, you've escaped
Being put up on a cross to feed the crows."
"I'm a good and worthy person!" One of my neighbors
Down here in the country would shake his head and say,
"Well, I don't know about that." The hawk is afraid
Of being caught in the snare; the wolf is afraid
Of falling into the pit; the fish is afraid
Of getting the hook caught in its mouth, but those
Who are truly good love goodness because
They love it, and hate wrongdoing. The *so-called* good man's
Afraid of punishment; if he saw a chance
Of getting away with it, he'd rub out the line
That separates the sacred from the profane.
If I had a thousand bushels of beans and you
Stole only one, I wouldn't be greatly harmed,
But theft would still be a sin, and you the thief.
That man I spoke of, so good in the eyes of the public,
In the Forum or in the law courts, loudly cries out,
When he offers an ox or pig in sacrifice
To propitiate the gods, "O Father Janus!"
Or loudly cries, "Apollo!," but under his breath
He prays to the goddess of thieves, "O goddess fair!
O fair Laverna, keep me from getting caught!
Preserve my reputation; hide my sins
In the dark of night, conceal them in a cloud!"

I find it hard to say how the greedy man
Is less a slave than the slave, when, slave to his nature,

in triviis fixum cum se demittit ob assem,
non video. nam qui cupiet, metuet quoque; porro,
qui metuens vivet, liber mihi non erit umquam.
perdidit arma, locum Virtutis deseruit, qui
semper in augenda festinat et obruitur re.
vendere cum possis captivum, occidere noli;
serviet utiliter: sine pascat durus aretque,
naviget ac mediis hiemet mercator in undis,
annonae prosit, portet frumenta penusque.

Vir bonus et sapiens audebit dicere: 'Pentheu,
rector Thebarum, quid me perferre patique
indignum coges?' 'adimam bona.' 'nempe pecus, rem,
lectos, argentum: tollas licet.' 'in manicis et
compedibus saevo te sub custode tenebo.'
'ipse deus, simul atque volam, me solvet.' opinor,
hoc sentit, 'moriar.' mors ultima linea rerum est.

He stoops and tries and tries to pinch a penny
Loose from the pavement some kid has soldered it to.
Anxiety owns the man who is owned by greed;
He whom anxiety owns is therefore a slave.
The man who is driven and overwhelmed by the need
For money, more and more of it, is a deserter
From virtue's ranks, having abandoned his weapons.
When you have the choice of killing or selling a captive,
Don't kill him, sell him—he'll be a useful slave,
If he's fit for the work, perhaps as shepherd or field hand,
Or maybe be sent to sea on a merchant ship
Making its way through heavy waves in the winter,
Or he'll carry crates of produce around in the market.

The wise and virtuous man will dare to say,
"Pentheus, king of Thebes, what is it that
You have in mind to do to make me suffer?"
"I'll take away all you own." "Do you mean by that
My cattle? My farm? My household goods? My spoons?
Take them and welcome." "I'll bind you hand and foot,
Shackled in chains and watched by a heartless jailer."
"Then God, with my consent, will set me free."
In my opinion, he means he's going to die.
Death is the finish line that everyone crosses.

Quamvis, Scaeva, satis per te tibi consulis et scis
quo tenuem pacto deceat maioribus uti,
disce docendus adhuc quae censet amiculus, ut si
caecus iter monstrare velit; tamen aspice si quid
et nos quod cures proprium fecisse loquamur.

Si te grata quies et primam somnus in horam
delectat, si te pulvis strepitusque rotarum,
si laedit caupona, Ferentinum ire iubebo.
nam neque divitibus contingunt gaudia solis
nec vixit male qui natus moriensque fefellit.
si prodesse tuis pauloque benignius ipsum
te tractare voles, accedes siccus ad unctum.
'si pranderet holus patienter, regibus uti
nollet Aristippus.' 'si sciret regibus uti,
fastidiret holus qui me notat.' utrius horum
verba probes et facta doce, vel iunior audi

i.17

TO SCAEVA

Scaeva, I know you know very well how to deal
With your own affairs; you know how to handle
The great ones of the world. Nevertheless,
Please listen to what I think—although, I admit,
I still have a lot to learn. It's a case, perhaps,
Of the blind leading the blind. But you can decide
If what I have to say is of any use.

If all you want in life is peace and quiet,
Snoozing the night away till the sun comes up,
Far from the hubbub and chatter of city taverns
And far from the dust and racket of city traffic,
By all means get away to little humble
Quiet boring Ferentinum. It's true,
The worldly don't have the answer to everything.
You could perfectly well let a whole life pass like this,
From birth to death, unnoticed by anyone.
But if you want to be a little kinder
Both to yourself and your friends, be willing to go
To dinner once in a while at a rich man's house.

A Cynic said to Aristippus, "If you
Were satisfied with cabbage for your dinner,
You'd have no reason to spend your time with princes."
And Aristippus replied, "If you knew how
To spend your time with princes, you wouldn't deign
To dine on cabbage." Now, which of these two
Is the one whose advice you should listen to? Or else,
You being junior to me, let *me* tell *you*

cur sit Aristippi potior sententia; namque
mordacem Cynicum sic eludebat, ut aiunt:
'scurror ego ipse mihi, populo tu; rectius hoc et
splendidius multo est. equus ut me portet, alat rex,
officium facio: tu poscis vilia rerum,
dante minor, quamvis fers te nullius egentem.'
omnis Aristippum decuit color et status et res,
temptantem maiora, fere praesentibus aequum:
contra, quem duplici panno patientia velat,
mirabor vitae via si conversa decebit.
alter purpureum non exspectabit amictum,
quidlibet indutus celeberrima per loca vadet
personamque feret non inconcinnus utramque;
alter Mileti textam cane peius et angui
vitabit chlanidem; morietur frigore, si non
rettuleris pannum. refer et sine vivat ineptus.

Res gerere et captos ostendere civibus hostis
attingit solium Iovis et caelestia temptat:
principibus placuisse viris non ultima laus est.
'non cuivis homini contingit adire Corinthum.'
sedit qui timuit ne non succederet. 'esto.
quid qui pervenit fecitque viriliter?' atqui
hic est aut nusquam quod quaerimus. hic onus horret

Why Aristippus's view is the better one.
This, so they say, is how Aristippus eluded
The snapping teeth of the Cynic: "My dinner table
Wit and satirical jokes are for my sake;
You do your thing for people on the street.
My way is better and far more elegant.
I do my thing to have a horse to ride
And to have a prince supply me with my food.
You beg for pennies and thus you make yourself
Inferior to whomever you get some from,
Although your boast is that you're not dependent
On anyone at all." For Aristippus
Could suit himself to any situation
Though, given the choice, he'd always choose the better.
On the other hand, I wonder if the man
Clothed in the rags that Cynics always wear
Would be *able* to deal with a better circumstance?
Aristippus wouldn't require a purple robe;
He'd make his elegant way through the crowded streets
Wearing whatever there happened to be at hand.
The other man would look at a nice warm cloak
Made out of beautiful cloth from Miletus as if
He thought it was much much worse than a dog or a snake.
You'd have to give him back his beggar's rags
Or he'd die of the cold. So, give him back his rags,
And leave him alone to lead his foolish life.

Those who perform heroic deeds of war
And bring their captives home to show to the crowd
Have reached the skies and touched the throne of Jove;
But he who has learned to please such men as these
Has not achieved the very least of things.

"That may be so, but tell me, can the one
Who has learned to please the foremost men, can he
Do it with his integrity intact?"

That's just the point that needs to be considered:
Not everyone has won his way to Corinth;

ut parvis animis et parvo corpore maius:
hic subit et perfert. aut virtus nomen inane est
aut decus et pretium recte petit experiens vir.

Coram rege sua de paupertate tacentes
plus poscente ferent distat sumasne pudenter
an rapias; atqui rerum caput hoc erat, hic fons.
'indotata mihi soror est, paupercula mater
et fundus nec vendibilis nec pascere firmus'
qui dicit, clamat 'victum date.' succinit alter
'et mihi!' dividuo findetur munere quadra.
sed tacitus pasci si posset corvus, haberet
plus dapis et rixae multo minus invidiaeque.
Brundisium comes aut Surrentum ductus amoenum
qui queritur salebras et acerbum frigus et imbris
aut cistam effractam et subducta viatica plorat,
nota refert meretricis acumina, saepe catellam
saepe periscelidem raptam sibi flentis, uti mox
nulla fides damnis verisque doloribus adsit.

Some have just sat still, afraid to try;
One man's afraid the burden's too heavy for him,
His soul and body too small to take it up;
The other takes it up and carries it through.
Manhood is just an empty word unless
The man who seeks what's valid to win, and does so
With dignity and style, is truly a man.
The man who, face to face with his patron, doesn't
Make a big issue about his needs and how
Bad off he is will do much better than
The man who begs. It makes a difference whether
A gift is accepted with modesty and decorum
Or grabbed at rapaciously. The style is what counts.
"Alas, alas, the family farm won't yield
Enough for us to live on; and nobody wants
To buy it; then too, my little sister's got
No dowry and my poor old mother's broke."
If you talk like that you'll sound exactly like
A panhandler on the street to the passerby.
"Feed me, oh feed me!" and right away then, of course,
Another one cries, "Feed me, oh feed me too!"
And pretty soon whatever there is to give
Is divided up into all too little parts.
But if the crow fed quietly by itself
It would have enough to eat, and more than enough,
Without the noisy quarreling and the envy.

He who accompanies his patron to
Brundisium or beautiful Sorrento
And spends his time complaining about the roads
And the cold and the rain and his luggage broken into
And his things being pilfered and so on and so on is like
Somebody's girlfriend weeping so often and so
Copiously about such things as the loss
Of a pretty necklace or anklet or some other trifle
That when she really has something to cry about,
Some genuine loss or trouble, nobody bothers
To pay the least attention. The person who's been

nec semel irrisus triviis attollere curat
fracto crure planum, licet illi plurima manet
lacrima, per sanctum iuratus dicat Osirim
'credite, non ludo: crudeles, tollite claudum!'
'quaere peregrinum' vicinia rauca reclamat.

Taken in once is never going to be
Taken in twice by a weeping beggar sporting
A putative broken leg, down at the crossroads,
Swearing by holy Osiris, crying out, "Oh,
Help me, help me, cruel people, help me!
Believe me, believe me, I'm not fooling, help me!"
And the neighborhood people holler back at him,
"Oh yeah? Go tell your story to a stranger!"

Si bene te novi, metues, liberrime Lolli,
scurrantis speciem praebere, professus amicum.
ut matrona meretrici dispar erit atque
discolor, infido scurrae distabit amicus.
est huic diversum vitio vitium prope maius,
asperitas agrestis et inconcinna gravisque,
quae se commendat tonsa cute, dentibus atris,
dum vult libertas dici mera veraque virtus.
virtus est medium vitiorum et utrimque reductum.
alter in obsequium plus aequo pronus et imi
derisor lecti sic nutum divitis horret,
sic iterat voces et verba cadentia tollit,
ut puerum saevo credas dictata magistro
reddere vel partis mimum tractare secundas.
alter rixatur de lana saepe caprina
propugnat nugis armatus: 'scilicet ut non
sit mihi prima fides?' et 'vere quod placet ut non
acriter elatrem? pretium aetas altera sordet.'
ambigitur quid enim? Castor sciat an Docilis plus,
Brundisium Minuci melius via ducat an Appi.

TO LOLLIUS MAXIMUS

I know how frank and forthright you are, dear Lollius,
So I'm sure you wouldn't want anyone you've sworn
Your friendship to to think you're a flatterer.
Flatterers and true friends resemble each other
No more than whores and wives. But the opposite vice
Is at least as bad as the vice of flattery:
Uncouth rudeness, awkward and obnoxious,
Proud of its bad breath and close-cropped hair,
Thinking they're signs of good old honest virtue.
But virtue situates itself between
Contrary extremes, as far as it can be
From one without inclining to the other.
One man, servile by nature, nothing but
A dinner-table buffoon of the lowest order,
Trembles whenever he sees the rich man's nod,
Echoes his words, picking them up as they fall
Under the table. You'd think he was a scared
Schoolboy reciting his lessons to his teacher,
Or like the second actor in the play,
Miming line by line the words of the first.
The other kind of man is ready to go
Ballistic over which kind of goat wool's better.
"Who says I'm wrong? Shut up and listen! Don't tell *me*
To keep my voice down!" And what's all this about?
Is Castor a better fighter than Dolichos?
Which way is better for getting to Brundisium?
Should you go by the Appian or the Mincian?

The rich man (though really he's maybe ten times worse)
Is inclined to look down on the man who spends every penny

Quem damnosa Venus, quem praeceps alea nudat,
gloria quem supra viris et vestit et unguit,
quem tenet argenti sitis importuna famesque,
quem paupertatis pudor et fuga, dives amicus,
saepe decem vitiis instructior, odit et horret,
aut si non odit, regit ac veluti pia mater
plus quam se sapere et virtutibus esse priorem
vult et ait prope vera: 'meae (contendere noli)
stultitiam patiuntur opes: tibi parvula res est.
arta decet sanum comitem toga; desine mecum
certare.' Eutrapelus cuicumque nocere volebat
vestimenta dabat pretiosa: 'beatus enim iam
cum pulchris tunicis sumet nova consilia et spes,
dormiet in lucem, scorto postponet honestum
officium, nummos alienos pascet, ad imum
Thrax erit aut holitoris aget mercede caballum.'

Arcanum neque tu scrutaberis illius umquam
commissumque teges et vino tortus et ira;
nec tua laudabis studia aut aliena reprendes,
nec cum venari volet ille, poemata panges.
gratia sic fratrum geminorum, Amphionis atque
Zethi, dissiluit, donec suspecta severo
conticuit lyra. fraternis cessisse putatur
moribus Amphion: tu cede potentis amici
lenibus imperiis, quotiensque educet in agros
Aeoliis onerata plagis iumenta canesque,
surge et inhumanae senium depone Camenae,
cenes ut pariter pulmenta laboribus empta.

He has to his name on women or gambling, or
Because the shame of not having much makes him spend
Much more than he should on getting all dressed up,
Perfumed, and coiffed far beyond his means. Or if
The rich man doesn't exactly despise the other,
He tries to set him straight and treats him the way
A hovering mother endeavors to make her child
A wiser and better person than she. He says
(And there's truth in what he says): "My money gives me
Plenty of leeway for folly—don't even think
About trying to be like me—you're much too poor.
The plainest toga is right for a sensible person
Who knows what his income is." Eutrapelus had
The right idea about how to ruin somebody:
"Just give him some fancy clothes. He'll put on the clothes
And put on a new idea of who he is:
He'll sleep till noon; he'll spend all his time with whores;
He'll pile up debts, and end up who knows what,
A grocery wagon driver, a gladiator."

Don't be too eager to know whatever secrets
Your patron has, but if he confides in you,
Then you must be sure to keep them to yourself,
Even if tortured to tell, say by anger, or wine.
Don't try to impose your own agenda on others,
And don't be disdainful of theirs. If your patron wants
To go out hunting, don't stay home because
You want to write a poem. The bond between
The Theban twins was nearly broken that way,
Till Amphion's lyre fell silent, because, they say,
He closed his music down in deference to
His brother's stern displeasure at such pleasure.
Just so, when your patron goes off into the fields,
With wagons, and mules, and hunting nets, and dogs,
Yield to his wishes, get up and gladly go,
And leave behind the unsociable grumpy Muse,
And join the others at the hunters' table
To eat the meat that was got with so much sweat.

Romanis sollemne viris opus, utile famae
vitaeque et membris, praesertim cum valeas et
vel cursu superare canem vel viribus aprum
possis. adde virilia quod speciosius arma
non est qui tractet: scis quo clamore coronae
proelia sustineas campestria; denique saevam
militiam puer et Cantabrica bella tulisti
sub duce qui templis Parthorum signa refigit
nunc, et si quid abest Italorum adiudicat arvis.
ac ne te retrahas et inexcusabilis absis,
quamvis nil extra numerum fecisse modumque
curas, interdum nugaris rure paterno;
partitur lintris exercitus, Actia pugna
te duce per pueros hostili more refertur;
adversarius est frater, lacus Hadria, donec
alterutrum velox Victoria fronde coronet.
consentire suis studiis qui crediderit te,
fautor utroque tuum laudabit pollice ludum.

Protinus ut moneam, si quid monitoris eges tu,
quid, de quoque viro, et cui dicas saepe videto.
percontatorem fugito; nam garrulus idem est
nec retinent patulae commissa fideliter aures,
et semel emissum volat irrevocabile verbum.
non ancilla tuum iecur ulceret ulla puerve
intra marmoreum venerandi limen amici,
ne pueri dominus pulchri caraeve puellae
munere te parvo beet aut incommodus angat.

The hunt after all is a solemn ritual
For Roman men, useful for reputation,
Good for the body—especially when *you're*
Fast as a hunting dog, and strong as a boar.
Nobody handles weapons as well as you,
And you've heard the admiring cheers and applause of the crowd
As they watch you prevail in the bouts on the Campus Martius.
When you were just a kid you fought in the rough
Cantabrian campaigns, under a leader
Who as I speak is bringing back to us
The Roman battle standards from where they hung
High in the arrogant temples of the Parthians,
And is prepared with Roman arms to conquer
Whatever still remains to fall to us.
And furthermore, though of course you're careful to be
A mild and pacific person, nevertheless
There are times when you like to play certain kinds of games.
Out at your father's summer place in the country,
You and your slaves perform the Actian battle.
Your little pond's the Adriatic Sea,
Your brother pretends to be your enemy,
The little family boats are the hostile fleets,
And the battle is on, till one of you wins the laurel.

To go on with my advice (that is, supposing
You need advice from me): Be careful about
The things you say and the people to whom you say them.
Avoid the man who asks too many questions.
No question but he'll be a teller of tales;
An ear that eager can't keep a secret for long,
And once a word slips out it won't come back.
I advise you not to fall for a boy or girl
Who belongs to your respected patron's household.
He might possibly make you a gift of the pretty boy
Or the pretty girl, and that might be pretty much
The only present you'll ever get from him;
Or else, displeased, he might refuse and thus
Cause you a lot of needless anguished longing.

qualem commendes etiam atque etiam aspice, ne mox
incutiant aliena tibi peccata pudorem.
fallimur et quondam non dignum tradimus: ergo,
quem sua culpa premet, deceptus omitte tueri,
ut penitus notum, si temptent crimina, serves
tuterisque tuo fidenter praesidio; qui
dente Theonino cum circumroditur, ecquid
ad te post paulo ventura pericula sentis?
nam tua res agitur paries cum proximus ardet
et neglecta solent incendia sumere viris.

Dulcis inexpertis cultura potentis amici:
expertus metuet. tu, dum tua navis in alto est,
hoc age, ne mutata retrorsum te ferat aura.
oderunt hilarem tristes tristemque iocosi,
sedatum celeres, agilem navumque remissi,
potores bibuli media de nocte Falerni
oderunt porrecta negantem pocula, quamvis
nocturnos iures te formidare tepores.
deme supercilio nubem; plerumque modestus
occupat obscuri speciem, taciturnus acerbi.

Inter cuncta leges et percontabere doctos
qua ratione queas traducere leniter aevum,
ne te semper inops agitet vexetque cupido,

Think more than twice before you introduce
Someone you know into the social group.
If he by any chance does something shameful,
The shame of it might then devolve on you.
Once in a while a mistake is made and someone
Who isn't worthy of getting in gets in.
When he goes wrong, if you were the one he tricked,
Don't bother to defend him. If somebody else,
Whom you know well, is wrongly accused of something,
You'll want to be his credible defender,
His bastion and his guardian protector,
For if he's bitten by Theon's slanderous tooth,
You'd better watch out, you could get bitten too.
Your own house is in danger when your neighbor's
House is on fire; a fire not watched can spread.

The cultivation of powerful friends is sweet
To those who haven't tried it; those who've tried it
Regard it with apprehension and with fear.
Be careful when your ship is out on the waters,
The wind may suddenly turn and carry you back.
The lighthearted hate the grave, the grave the lighthearted;
The diligent hate the lazy, the lazy hate
Those who are early risers, up and at it;
Drinkers hate those who beg off drinking with them,
Saying they can't because it spoils their sleep.
And the very look on one's face can be misread:
The shy person's serious look can be mistaken
For an ominous secretive look; the shy person's silence
For ominous close-mouthed malice.

                                        Amid all this,
Interrogate the writings of the wise,
Asking them to tell you how you can
Get through your life in a peaceable tranquil way.
Will it be greed, that always feels poverty-stricken,
That harasses and torments you all your days?
Will it be hope and fear about trivial things,

neu pavor et rerum mediocriter utilium spes;
virtutem doctrina paret naturane donet;
quid minuat curas, quid te tibi reddat amicum;
quid pure tranquillet, honos an dulce lucellum
an secretum iter et fallentis semita vitae.

Me quotiens reficit gelidus Digentia rivus,
quem Mandela bibit, rugosus frigore pagus,
quid sentire putas? quid credis, amice, precari?
sit mihi quod nunc est, etiam minus, et mihi vivam
quod superest aevi, si quid superesse volunt di;
sit bona librorum et provisae frugis in annum
copia, neu fluitem dubiae spe pendulus horae.

Sed satis est orare Iovem quae ponit et aufert:
det vitam, det opes. aequum mi animum ipse parabo.

In anxious alternation in your mind?
Where is it virtue comes from, is it from books?
Or is it a gift from Nature that can't be learned?
What is the way to become a friend to yourself?
What brings tranquillity? What makes cares less?
Honor? Or money? Or living your life unnoticed?
Whenever I drink from the cold refreshing waters
Of the little brook Digentia, down below
Our local hill town, what do you think I pray for?
"May I continue to have what I have right now,
Or even less, as long as I'm self-sufficient.
If the gods should grant me life, though just for a while,
May I live my life to myself, with books to read,
And food to sustain me through another year,
And not to waver with the wavering hours."
But maybe it's enough to pray to Jove,
Who has the power to give and take away,
Simply for life and for the means of life;
I will myself provide a steadfast mind.

Prisco si credis, Maecenas docte, Cratino,
nulla placere diu nec vivere carmina possunt
quae scribuntur aquae potoribus. ut male sanos
ascripsit Liber Satyris Faunisque poetas;
vina fere dulces oluerunt mane Camenae.
laudibus arguitur vini vinosus Homerus.
Ennius ipse pater numquam nisi potus ad arma
prosiluit dicenda. 'Forum Putealque Libonis
mandabo siccis, adimam cantare severis:'
hoc simul edixi, non cessavere poetae
nocturno certare mero, putere diurno.
quid? si quis vultu torvo ferus et pede nudo
exiguaeque togae simulet textore Catonem,
virtutemne repraesentet moresque Catonis?
rupit Iarbitam Timagenis aemula lingua,
dum studet urbanus tenditque disertus haberi.
decipit exemplar vitiis imitabile. quod si
pallerem casu, biberent exsangue cuminum.

i.19

TO MAECENAS

If you believe what you read in old Cratinus,
Well-read Maecenas, you know there's not one poem
That gives a reader lasting pleasure which
A water-bibber wrote. Ever since Bacchus
Enrolled us poets among his fauns and satyrs,
There's been a hint of the memory of wine
On the morning breath of the Muses. Homer shows,
By the way he praises wine, what a drinker he was;
Old father Ennius was never known to step
Forward loudly praising heroic deeds
Without having knocked a couple back beforehand.
"I assign the sober a seat by Libo's Well,
And I forbid teetotalers to sing."
Ever since the day when I laid down this law,
Bards have competed nightly in how much wine
They could drink, and daily in how they stink of it.

What do you think, if somebody went around
Barefoot, and wearing a skimpy toga, and
A fearsome gloomy wild-beast look like Cato,
He'd therefore *be* like virtuous moral Cato?
Iarbitas' tongue blew up on him when he tried
To imitate Timagenes' oh so smoothly
Flowing urbane eloquence of style.
How easy it is for the copyable faults
Of an estimable model to lead astray.
Suppose I turn a little pale for a moment:
These mimics of me would right away take to drinking
Some potion that causes pallor. A servile bunch—

O imitatores, servum pecus, ut mihi saepe
bilem, saepe iocum vestri movere tumultus!
libera per vacuum posui vestigia princeps,
non aliena meo pressi pede. qui sibi fidet,
dux reget examen. Parios ego primus iambos
ostendi Latio, numeros animosque secutus
Archilochi, non res et agentia verba Lycamben.
ac ne me foliis ideo brevioribus ornes
quod timui mutare modos et carminis artem,
temperat Archilochi Musam pede mascula Sappho,
temperat Alcaeus, sed rebus et ordine dispar,
nec socerum quaerit quem versibus oblinat atris,
nec sponsae laqueum famoso carmine nectit.
hunc quoque, non alio dictum prius ore, Latinus
vulgavi fidicen. iuvat immemorata ferentem
ingenuis oculisque legi manibusque teneri.

Scire velis mea cur ingratus opuscula lector
laudet ametque domi, premat extra limen iniquus?
non ego ventosae plebis suffragia venor
impensis cenarum et tritae munere vestis;
non ego nobilium scriptorum auditor et ultor
grammaticas ambire tribus et pulpita dignor.
hinc illae lacrimae. 'spissis indigna theatris
scripta pudet recitare et nugis addere pondus'

Sometimes they make me angry, with all their fuss,
And other times they only make me laugh.

I was the first to tread untrodden ground;
I would not go where others had gone before.
He who believes in himself will lead the pack.
I was the first to bring to Italy
The music of Archilochus of Paros,
His rhythms and what they were capable of, but not
The things he said to hunt Lycambes down.
And if the fact that I showed such respect
For another's forms and meters should influence you
To crown me with a skimpier wreath, consider
How manly Sappho regulates her verse
According to Archilochéan rhythms;
Alcaeus, too, although he diverges far
In his agenda, having no father-in-law
To be vindictive against with smearing words,
Having no motive to weave with libelous language
A noose with which his bride would hang herself.
It was I, playing the Latin lyre, who was
The first to bring Alcaeus into Latium;
No other had sung that music here before,
And I rejoice that in my book I brought
Something really new to intelligent readers.

Do you want to know the reason my thankless reader,
Who loves and praises my poems when he's at home,
Disparages them in public? I'm not like one
Of those politicians who tries to buy the votes
Of capricious citizens by throwing big parties
And offering generous gifts of (secondhand) clothes.
I'm not the kind who goes to a lot of readings
And then, to take revenge, do my best myself
To woo the tribe of critics by reading too.
If I should say, "I'd be embarrassed to read
My unworthy stuff in a crowded hall and add
Another nothing to the pile," someone would say,

si dixi, 'rides' ait 'et Iovis auribus ista
servas: fidis enim manare poetica mella
te solum, tibi pulcher.' ad haec ego naribus uti
formido et, luctantis acuto ne secer ungui,
'displicet iste locus' clamo et diludia posco.
ludus enim genuit trepidum certamen et iram,
ira truces inimicitias et funebre bellum.

"You can't kid me. You're saving up your stuff
To read to Jove. You're stuck on yourself. You think
You're the only one, the only one, from whom
The true honey of poetry drips and flows."
I'm afraid of turning up my nose at this
And afraid in this wrestling match of being scratched
By his sharp nails, and so I say, "Well, this
Just isn't the time or place," and I call for time-out.
Games like this are a cause of anxiety
And anger, and anger causes quarreling,
And all of it could end in a war to the death.

Vertumnum Ianumque, liber, spectare videris,
scilicet ut prostes Sosiorum pumice mundus.
odisti clavis et grata sigilla pudico;
paucis ostendi gemis et communia laudas,
non ita nutritus. fuge quo descendere gestis.
non erit emisso reditus tibi. 'quid miser egi?
quid volui?' dices, ubi quid te laeserit et scis
in breve te cogi, cum plenus languet amator.

Quod si non odio peccantis desipit augur,
carus eris Romae donec te deserat aetas.
contrectatus ubi manibus sordescere vulgi
coeperis, aut tineas pasces taciturnus inertis
aut fugies Uticam aut vinctus mitteris Ilerdam.
ridebit monitor non exauditus, ut ille
qui male parentem in rupis protrusit asellum
iratus: quis enim invitum servare laboret?

i.20

TO HIS BOOK

My book, you look to me as if you're longing
To get yourself down to Janus and Vertumnus
And put yourself on sale, all pumiced and ready.
I know you hate the idea that modesty loves,
Of being locked away from people's gaze.
You want to be available to the many,
Not just the few. You weren't brought up that way.

But off you go, down where you're itching to go.
There's just one thing I want you to remember:
Once you're out there, there is no coming back.
"What have I done? What was I thinking of?"
That's what we'll hear you cry, your feelings hurt,
After your lover has had enough of you
And packs you off somewhere in a dusty closet.

But unless my disapproval of your behavior
Undoes my prophetic powers, here's what will happen:
You will be dear to Rome till your youth goes by.
Having been soiled by all those pawing hands,
You'll either lie in silence while the moths,
That cannot read, will feed on you, or else
You'll make your way to far-off Africa
Or be tied up and sent away to Spain.

Your guardian then, to whom you wouldn't listen,
Will have the last laugh, like the man whose donkey
Kept pulling against being pulled back from the very
Edge of a cliff, till finally the man

hoc quoque te manet, ut pueros elementa docentem
occupet extremis in vicis balba senectus.

Cum tibi sol tepidus pluris admoverit auris,
me libertino natum patre et in tenui re
maiores pennas nido extendisse loqueris,
ut quantum generi demas virtutibus addas;
me primis urbis belli placuisse domique;
corporis exigui, praecanum, solibus aptum,
irasci celerem, tamen ut placabilis essem.
forte meum si quis te percontabitur aevum,
me quater undenos sciat implevisse Decembris
collegam Lepidum quo dixit Lollius anno.

Lost patience and pushed the stupid thing right over.
Why save a creature that doesn't want to be saved?

And after all that you'll end up in a school
Far from any city, God knows where,
A babbling poor old man, trying to teach
Young boys in a little school their ABC's.

But when the day is nearly done, and people
Are sitting around you, taking the evening air,
Please tell them who I was: son of a freedman,
In humble circumstance, my wings too strong
For the nest I was born in. What your tale subtracts
Because of my birth may it add because of my merit—
The foremost men of Rome, in peace and war,
Were pleased with me and what I was able to do;
A little man, and prematurely gray,
A lover of the sun; easily angered,
But easily pacified. If anyone asks,
I was forty-four years old in that December
When Lollius chose Lepidus as his partner.

BOOK TWO

Cum tot sustineas et tanta negotia solus,
res Italas armis tuteris, moribus ornes,
legibus emendes, in publica commoda peccem,
si longo sermone morer tua tempora, Caesar.

Romulus et Liber pater et cum Castore Pollux,
post ingentia facta deorum in templa recepti,
dum terras hominumque colunt genus, aspera bella
componunt, agros assignant, oppida condunt,
ploravere suis non respondere favorem
speratum meritis. diram qui contudit Hydram
notaque fatali portenta labore subegit,
comperit invidiam supremo fine domari.
urit enim fulgore suo qui praegravat artis
infra se positas: exstinctus amabitur idem.
praesenti tibi maturos largimur honores
iurandasque tuum per numen ponimus aras,
nil oriturum alias, nil ortum tale fatentes.
sed tuus hoc populus sapiens et iustus in uno,
te nostris ducibus, te Grais anteferendo,
cetera nequaquam simili ratione modoque
aestimat et, nisi quae terris semota suisque

TO AUGUSTUS

You bear the burden alone of so many things:
Keeping Rome safe from harm with your guardian armies;
Improving her laws; establishing new rules
Of civilized behavior. I would be guilty
Of interference with the public good
If I kept you from your business with too long talk.

Romulus, Father Liber, and Castor and Pollux,
Who cared for men and for their dwelling places,
Settled their savage wars, apportioned their fields,
Raised up their cities, performed these deeds so greatly
That they were granted seats among the gods,
And yet they found that the gratitude of men
Was incommensurate measured by what they did;
And Hercules who killed the terrible Hydra
And so many other monsters discovered that only
Death was able to slay the monster Envy.
The man whose brilliant merits far outshine
The merits of those below him scorches them.
Not till his light goes out will he be loved.
Yet, Caesar Augustus, in your lifetime we
Bestow on you your early-ripened honors,
Raise altars in order to swear by Caesar's name,
Acknowledge that heretofore no one like you
Has risen, and none like you will rise again.
And yet your people, having in this instance
Shown that they were capable of such wisdom
In giving precedence to you above
Our Roman leaders in our past and also

temporibus defuncta videt, fastidit et odit,
sic fautor veterum ur tabulas peccare vetantis
quas bis quinque viri sanxerunt, foedera regum
vel Gabiis vel cum rigidis aequata Sabinis,
pontificum libros, annosa volumina vatum
dictitet Albano Musas in monte locutas.

Si, quia Graiorum sunt antiquissima quaeque
scripta vel optima, Romani pensantur eadem
scriptores trutina, non est quod multa loquamur:
nil intra est olea, nil extra est in nuce duri.
venimus ad summum fortunae: pingimus atque
psallimus et luctamur Achivis doctius unctis?

Si meliora dies, ut vina, poemata reddit,
scire velim chartis pretium quotus arroget annus.
scriptor abhinc annos centum qui decidit, inter
perfectos veteresque referri debet an inter
vilis atque movos? excludat iurgia finis.
'est vetus atque probus centum qui perficit annos.'
quid qui deperiit minor uno mense vel anno?
inter quos referendus erit? veteresne probosque
an quos et praesens et postera respuat aetas?
'iste quidem veteres inter ponetur honeste
qui vel mense brevi vel toto est iunior anno.'
utor permisso caudaeque pilos ut equinae
paulatim vello et demo unum, demo etiam unum,
dum cadat elusus ratione ruentis acervi
qui redit ad fastos et virtutem aestimat annis
miraturque nihil nisi quod Libitina sacravit.

The leaders of the Greeks who came before them,
Seem to judge other things quite differently,
Rejecting, scorning, everything that hasn't
Lived out its days on earth long since, and gone.
They favor all these old old things so much
They swear the Tables that the Ten Men wrote,
Old treaties with the Gabii or the Sabines,
The daybooks of the Pontiffs, the prophecies
Preserved in ancient scrolls, were, one and all,
The sacred sayings of the Alban Muses.

If, just because we know that of the Greeks
The earliest writers are best, we therefore use
The same set of scales to compare them with our writers,
What's the result? "Why, that nut has no shell!"
"That olive has no pit!" Just because we've prospered,
And conquered everything and gotten rich,
Are we supposed to think that we can paint
As well as the ancient Greeks could paint, or play
The cithara, or wrestle, as skillfully?
If poetry, like wine, improves with age,
Then tell me, I'd like to know, how do you know
Exactly in what year a particular poem
Turns into a good one? Some writer, say, who died
A hundred years ago, is he ancient, and worthy,
Or modern, and worthless? There has to be a system.
You say, "If he died a hundred years ago,
He's good, being one of the ancients." But if he died
A month, or maybe a year, before that hundred,
Tell me, what then? One of the honored old?
Or a rank newcomer subject to our scorn?
If I accept your premise, it's like pulling
One hair out of the horse's tail, and then
Another, another, and so on and so on another,
To find out how many it takes to call it a tail.
He's bound to be baffled as the heap collapses,
Who counts by annals, grain by grain, and only
Esteems what the goddess of funerals sanctifies.

Ennius, et sapiens et fortis et alter Homerus,
ut critici dicunt, leviter curare videtur
quo promissa cadant et somnia Pythagorea.
Naevius in manibus non est et mentibus haeret
paene recens? adeo sanctum est vetus omne poema.
ambigitur quotiens, uter utro sit prior, aufert
Pacuvius docti famam senis, Accius alti,
dicitur Afrani toga convenisse Menandro,
Plautus ad exemplar Siculi properare Epicharmi,
vincere Caecilius gravitate, Terentius arte.
hos ediscit et hos arto stipata theatro
spectat Roma potens; habet hos numeratque poetas
ad nostrum tempus Livi scriptoris ab aevo.

Interdum vulgus rectum videt, est ubi peccat.
si veteres ita miratur laudatque poetas
ut nihil anteferat, nihil illis comparet, errat:
si quaedam nimis antique, si pleraque dure
dicere credit eos, ignave multa fatetur,
et sapit et mecum facit et Iove iudicat aequo.

Non equidem insector delendaque carmina Livi
esse reor, memini quae plagosum mihi parvo
Orbilium dictare; sed emendata videri
pulchraque et exactis minimum distantia miror,
inter quae verbum emicuit si forte decorum et
si versus paulo concinnior unus et alter,
iniuste totum ducit venditque poema.

Good brave old Ennius, whom the critics are
Pleased to refer to as "our second Homer,"
Doesn't show many signs of caring about
His Pythagoras-dream and its promise of being immortal.
So much revered is every ancient poem
That we keep Naevius present in our minds
"As if he wrote just yesterday"; we gravely
Discuss the question whether old Accius,
"His style so elevated," is better than old
Pacuvius, "so learnèd"; Afranius,
We say, "is fit to wear Menander's robe";
Plautus's dexterity is "just
Exactly like the dexterity of his model,
Sicily's Epicharmus"; Caecilius wins
The dignity prize; the art prize goes to Terence.
Proud Rome is proud to learn their lines by heart
And the theaters are packed to see their plays.
They are Rome's honor roll of poetry,
Remembered from Livius' time down to our own.

Sometimes people see straight, sometimes they don't.
If they marvel at and praise these ancient poets
As if they were nonpareils, of course they're wrong;
If they concede that these old writers sometimes
Sound very old-fashioned, sometimes rather clumsy,
And in stretches flat and boring, then they're right,
In agreement with my judgment and with Jove's.
Don't get me wrong. My purpose isn't to run
The poems of Livius, say, into the ground.
It isn't my intention to destroy them.
I remember how Orbilius, with his cane,
Used to thwack us in time to those verses in the schoolroom.
It's just that I'm surprised when they're regarded
As seamlessly beautiful, flawless, just about perfect.
Sometimes if there's a specially pleasing phrase
Or several specially well-constructed lines,
These will beguile the reader into thinking
The poem is successful all the way through.

indignor quidquam reprehendi, non quia crasse
compositum illepideve putetur, sed quia nuper,
nec veniam antiquis, sed honorem et praemia posci.
recte necne crocum floresque perambulet Attae
fabula si dubitem, clament periisse pudorem
cuncti paene patres, ea cum reprehendere coner
quae gravis Aesopus, quae doctus Roscius egit:
vel quia nil rectum nisi quod placuit sibi ducunt,
vel quia turpe putant parere minoribus et quae
imberbes didicere senes perdenda fateri.
iam Saliare Numae carmen qui laudat et illud
quod mecum ignorat solus vult scire videre,
ingeniis non ille favet plauditque sepultis,
nostra sed impugnat, nos nostraque lividus odit.

Quod si tam Graecis novitas invisa fuisset
quam nobis, quid nunc esset vetus? aut quid haberet
quod legeret tereretque viritim publicus usus?

Ut primum positis nugari Graecia bellis
coepit et in vitium Fortuna labier aequa,
nunc athletarum studiis, nunc arsit equorum,
marmoris aut eboris fabros aut aeris amavit,
suspendit picta vultum mentemque tabella,
nunc tibicinibus, nunc est gavisa tragoedis;
sub nutrice puella velut si luderet infans,
quod cupide petiit, mature plena reliquit.
quid placet aut odio est quod non mutabile credas?
hoc paces habuere bonae ventique secundi.

It makes me indignant when I hear a work
Blamed not because it's crude or graceless but
Only because it's new, and at the same time
The faults of some ancient work not being excused
But rather being granted unstinted praise.
And if I should question whether old Atta's feet
Stumble in all those flowers on his stage,
Or criticize the works in which the grave
Aesopus or the learned Roscius acted,
All the old men would cry that shame is dead.
Either they think that nothing could possibly please
Except what they've been pleased by, or they think
It's wrong to give in to the young and to admit,
When they are old, that what they learned when they
Were young and beardless might possibly have to go.
The man who praises Numa's Sicilian hymns,
And affects to understand what he understands
No better than I, is motivated not
By reverence for the genius of the past
But rather by scorn and hatred of the present.
Had the Greeks hated the new the way we do,
Whatever would have been able to grow to be old?
What would we have, to read and reread with delight,
Thumbing it through to find our favorite lines?

As soon as her wars were over and done with, Greece
Began to sink into triviality,
Foolish in her good fortune. She burned with passion
Now for athletes, now for horses; now
She fell in love with sculptors and their sculptures,
Ivory, marble, bronze; now she gazed
At the latest painter's painting, out of her mind
With rapture; rapturous now for a flutist,
And now for an actor on the tragic stage.
She was like a little child importuning
Her nurse to give her something that she wants,
And throwing it aside as soon as she has it.
Is there anything, do you think, that, being loved,

Romae dulce diu fuit et sollemne reclusa
mane domo vigilare, clienti promere iura,
cautos nominibus rectis expendere nummos,
maiores audire, minori dicere per quae
crescere res posset, minui damnosa libido.
mutavit mentem populus levis et calet uno
scribendi studio; pueri patresque severi
fronde comas vincti cenant et carmina dictant.
ipse ego, qui nullos me affirmo scribere versus,
invenior Parthis mendacior, et prius orto
sole vigil calamum et chartas et scrinia posco.
navem agere ignarus navis timet; habrotonum aegro
non audet nisi qui didicit dare; quod medicorum est
promittunt medici; tractant fabrilia fabri:
scribimus indocti doctique poemata passim.

Hic error tamen et levis haec insania quantas
virtutes habeat, sic collige: vatis avarus
non temere est animus; versus amat, hoc studet unum;
detrimenta, fugas servorum, incendia ridet;
non fraudem socio puerove incogitat ullam
pupillo; vivit siliquis et pane secundo;
militiae quamquam piger et malus, utilis urbi,
si das hoc, parvis quoque rebus magna iuvari.
os tenerum pueri balbumque poeta figurat,

Couldn't be hated soon, and vice versa?
Such were the fruits of peace and of fair weather.

The Romans used to like to get up early
And open their doors to let the fresh air in;
To call in what was owed them as soon as due;
To listen to the advice their elders gave them,
And give their juniors advice about how to save
And how to prosper and how to avoid giving in
To ruinous appetites and gratifications.
But times and tastes have changed. Now everyone
Is seized with the desire to write a poem;
Grave elders and their offspring crowned with wreaths
Dictate their verses to one another at dinner;
And as for me, I'm lying in my teeth
When I solemnly swear I've sworn off scribbling lines.
No sooner do I wake up than I call for a pen
And paper, and off I go. A man who knows nothing
About how to sail a ship won't do it; he's scared to.
Doctors do doctor's work. Carpenters handle
The tools it takes a carpenter's skills to use.
But skilled or unskilled we all feel free to write poems.

And yet in the end there's something to be said
For this kind of craze. It's relatively harmless,
And, more than that, it even has its virtues.
The poet isn't likely, after all,
To be money-mad; it's poetry he's mad for;
Financial ruin, runaway slaves, his house
Burned to the ground—none of this fazes him;
Swindling a partner or defrauding a ward
Couldn't be further from his mind; he doesn't
Care if he lives on gruel and day-old bread.
And though he certainly isn't much of a soldier,
He's of some use to his country, if you agree
That little contributions can promote
The greater good. His verses help the tender
Mouths of lisping children learn to speak,

torquet ab obscenis iam nunc sermonibus aurem,
mox etiam pectus praeceptis format amicis,
asperitatis et invidiae corrector et irae;
recte facta refert, orientia tempora notis
instruit exemplis, inopem solatur et aegrum.
castis cum pueris ignara puella mariti
disceret unde preces, vatem ni Musa dedisset?
poscit opem chorus et praesentia numina sentit,
caelestis implorat aquas, docta prece blandus,
avertit morbos, metuenda pericula pellit,
impetrat et pacem et locupletem frugibus annum.
carmine di superi placantur, carmine Manes.

Agricolae prisci, fortes parvoque beati,
condita post frumenta levantes tempore festo
corpus et ipsum animum spe finis dura ferentem,
cum sociis operum pueris et coniuge fida,
Tellurem porco, Silvanum lacte piabant,
floribus et vino Genium memorem brevis aevi.
Fescennina per hunc invecta licentia morem
versibus alternis opprobria rustica fudit.
libertasque recurrentis accepta per annos
lusit amabiliter, donec iam saevus apertam
in rabiem coepit verti iocus et per honestas
ire domos impune minax. doluere cruento
dente lacessiti; fuit intactis quoque cura
condicione super communi. quin etiam lex
poenaque lata, malo quae nollet carmine quemquam
describi. vertere modum formidine fustis
ad bene dicendum delectandumque redacti.

And then they teach them what's polite to say
And what is not; his gentle precepts shape
Their minds as they grow up, telling them famous
Examples of men who disciplined themselves
Against their own capacities for anger,
Envy, savage incivility.
The poet's verses comfort the weak and helpless,
And solace those who are bereft and grieving.
And how would chaste boys and unwed maidens learn
The suppliant hymn they sing, unless the Muse
Had granted them a poet? And as they sing,
They feel the listening presence of the gods,
To whom they pray for protection from the plague
And from all dreaded dangers from without;
In song they pray for rain to fall from heaven;
They pray for peace and for a fruitful harvest.
The gods above and the gods below are pleased.

Farmers in the old days, strong simple people,
At harvest home at last had holiday time,
For body and soul alike that had endured
Their labor in the hope of its getting done,
And with their wives, and slaves, and fellow workers
Made offerings to propitiate the gods,
Swine to Tellus the Earth, milk to Sylvanus,
Flowers and wine to each man's personal god
(Who knows how short or long his life will be).
On holidays like this the farm folk staged
Battles of taunting alternating song,
An annual game, all in innocent fun,
Until the game turned vicious, and, uncontrolled,
Prowled raging among the houses of honest people.
Those who were bitten by its teeth were outraged,
And others sympathized with them, and so
A law was promulgated that forbade,
On pain of punishment, the defamation
Of anyone in song. Men changed their ways,
For fear of being whipped, and thus ensued
More gentle and more civilized ways of speaking.

Graecia capta ferum victorem cepit et artis
intulit agresti Latio. sic horridus ille
defluxit numerus Saturnius et grave virus
munditiae pepulere; sed in longum tamen aevum
manserunt hodieque manent vestigia ruris.
serus enim Graecis admovit acumina chartis
et post Punica bella quietus quaerere coepit
quid Sophocles et Thespis et Aeschylus utile ferrent.
temptavit quoque rem, si digne vertere posset,
et placuit sibi, natura sublimis et acer;
nam spirat tragicum satis et feliciter audet,
sed turpem putat inscite metuitque lituram.

Creditur, ex medio quia res arcessit, habere
sudoris minimum sed habet comoedia tanto
plus oneris quanto veniae minus. aspice Plautus
quo pacto partis tutetur amantis ephebi,
ut patris attenti, lenonis ut insidiosi,
quantus sit Dossennus edacibus in parasitis,
quam non astricto percurrat pulpita socco.
gestit enim nummum in loculos demittere, post hoc
securus cadat an recto stet fabula talo.

Quem tulit ad scaenam ventoso Gloria curru,
exanimat lentus spectator, sedulus inflat;
sic leve, sic parvum est, animum quod laudis avarum
subruit aut reficit valeat res ludicra si me
palma negata macrum, donata reducit opimum!

Captive Greece took its Roman captor captive,
Invading uncouth Latium with its arts;
The fetid scum of the crude Saturnian meter
Was drained away and the water began to clear.
But vestiges of old savagery persisted,
And still persist, because the Roman writer
Was tardy in taking advantage of the best
Examples that the Greeks could offer him.
So it was only after the Punic Wars,
In the peace and quiet that followed, that he began
To ask how Aeschylus and Sophocles
And Thespis might be of use. He began to try
Experiments to see how worthily
He could perform, and he was often pleased,
Not without reason, being by nature full
Of energy and spirit, joyfully
Adventurous, and capable of being
Excited and inspired by tragic example,
But still half-trained and therefore scared to blot,
Thinking it shameful to have a second thought.

Comedy is regarded as much easier,
Its material being the stuff of common life;
But actually it's harder, it being harder
To get away with it. You get showed up.
Just look how Plautus does his usual thing:
The bawd, the lovesick swain, the suspicious father,
The sneering villain, the greedy parasites—
He pads about slipshod in his comic socks.
So long as he gets some money to put in his pocket
He couldn't care less if his play falls apart or not.

The poet whose ambition is to be carried
Onto the stage in Glory's airy chariot
Will feel he is borne aloft upon the applauding
Wings of the crowd's approval, if it approve;

And if it doesn't approve, he'll panic because
There are no clapping wings to hold him up.

saepe etiam audacem fugat hoc terretque poetam,
quod numero plures, virtute et honore minores,
indocti stolidique et depugnare parati
si discordet eques, media inter carmina poscunt
aut ursum aut pugiles; his nam plebecula gaudet.
verum equitis quoque iam migravit ab aure voluptas
omnis ad incertos oculos et gaudia vana.
quattuor aut pluris aulaea premuntur in horas,
dum fugiunt equitum turmae peditumque catervae;
mox trahitur manibus regum fortuna retortis,
esseda festinant, pilenta, petorrita, naves,
captivum portatur ebur, captiva Corinthus.
si foret in terris, rideret Democritus, seu
diversum confusa genus panthera camelo
sive elephans albus vulgi converteret ora;
spectaret populum ludis attentius ipsis,
ut sibi praebentem nimio spectacula plura;
scriptores autem narrare putaret asello
fabellam surdo. nam quae pervincere voces
evaluere sonum referunt quem nostra theatra?

So light, so little, is glory, so easily lost.
As far as I'm concerned, being a playwright
Is not for me, if happiness depends
On whether the audience claps for me or not.
Sometimes even the most self-confident
And strongest poet is scared, and scared away,
When the theatergoing mob in the back rows,
Right in the middle of his play's performance,
Calls out for bears or boxers, their kind of thing,
And they're ready to brawl with their front-rows betters about it.
And, as a matter of fact, their betters' pleasure,
Which used to derive from what the attentive ear
Could concentrate on, began to derive from what
The wandering wondering eye could be dazzled by.
Four hours or more the spectacle goes on:
Platoons of foot and troops of horse parading
Around the thundering stage as if they'd won;
Once fortunate kings unfortunate now, hands tied
Behind their backs, dragged on for the Roman crowd
To mock in triumph; all sorts of war machines,
War ships, war chariots, wagons loaded with
Ivory booty and loot of Corinthian bronze,
All lumbering about on the noisy platform.
If Democritus by any means came back
From the other world to this, he'd have a good laugh.
Whatever the eyes of the crowd were fixed upon
—Some hybrid monster, perhaps, half camel, half leopard,
Or an albino elephant—his gaze
Would be fixed much more attentively upon
The crowd itself than on the spectacle.
They'd give him more material for laughter.
As for the playwright and the playwright's words,
Democritus would think them meant for the ears
Of a stone-deaf donkey. For who could have a voice
That's strong enough to be heard in the uproar of
Our theaters today? You'd think you were caught in the roar
Of a storm in the Tuscan ocean, or in the roar
Of a tempest in the forest of Cape Garganus.

Garganum mugire putes nemus aut mare Tuscum,
tanto cum strepitu ludi spectantur et artes
divitiaeque peregrinae, quibus oblitus actor
cum stetit in scaena, concurrit dextera laevae.
dixit adhuc aliquid? nil sane. quid placet ergo?
lana Tarentino violas imitata veneno.

Ac ne forte putes me, quae facere ipse recusem,
cum recte tractent alii, laudare maligne,
ille per extentum funem mihi posse videtur
ire poeta, meum qui pectus inaniter angit,
irritat, mulcet, falsis terroribus implet,
et, magus ut, modo me Thebis, modo ponit Athenis.
verum age, et his qui se lectori credere malunt
quam spectatoris fastidia ferre superbi
curam redde brevem, si munus Apolline dignum
vis complere libris et vatibus addere calcar,
ut studio maiore petant Helicona virentem.
multa quidem nobis facimus mala saepe poetae
(ut vineta egomet caedam mea), cum tibi librum
sollicito damus aut fesso; cum laedimur, unum
si quis amicorum est ausus reprehendere versum;
cum loca iam recitata revolvimus irrevocati;

That's what the roaring is like in the theater when
The audience first sees the gorgeous set
And sees the foreign raiment the actor wears
When, lost in the raiment, he makes his appearance onstage.
Right hands crashingly come together with left hands.
"What was it he said?" "He hasn't said a word."
"Then what are they all applauding for?" "It's for
That marvelous Tarentine poisonous-violet costume."

But I wouldn't want you to think I'm unwilling to praise
Others for doing well what I myself
Don't want to do. For me the good playwright poet
Is like a marvelous high-wire acrobat who,
Walking on air, can scare me to death, and then
Momentarily calm me down, and then
Scare me to death all over again. He uses
Magic to make me suddenly be in Athens
And five minutes later find that I'm in Thebes.
Nevertheless those writers who prefer
To submit themselves to the judgment of a reader
Rather than undergo the vulgar scorn
Of the theatergoing crowd merit at least
A moment of your attention, if you desire
To fill the shelves of your Apollonian gift
With books that deserve to be there, and if you want
To urge your poets on to greater efforts
To climb the verdant sides of Helicon.
I must confess (though to do so is to slash
At my own grapevines), we poets often do
Great harm to ourselves—for instance, when you're weary
And distracted and we bother you with our poems;
Or when our feelings are hurt because a friend
Is brave enough to criticize so much
As a single line; when, uninvited to do so,
We recite all over again a poem or passage,
One of our own, that we'd just got through reciting;
When we lament the fact that people never
Notice how hard we work to create our poems,

cum lamentamur non apparere labores
nostros et tenui deducta poemata filo;
cum speramus eo rem venturam ut, simul atque
carmina rescieris nos fingere, commodus ultro
arcessas et egere vetes et scribere cogas.
sed tamen est operae pretium cognoscere qualis
aedituos habeat belli spectata domique
virtus, indigno non committenda poetae.
gratus Alexandro, regi magno, fuit ille
Choerilus, incultis qui versibus et male natis
rettulit acceptos, regale nomisma, Philippos.
sed veluti tractata notam labemque remittunt
atramenta, fere scriptores carmine foedo
splendida facta linunt. idem rex ille, poema
qui tam ridiculum tam care prodigus emit,
edicto vetuit ne quis se praeter Apellen
pingeret aut alius Lysippo duceret aera
fortis Alexandri vultum simulantia. quod si
iudicium subtile videndis artibus illud
ad libros et ad haec Musarum dona vocares,
Boeotum in crasso iurares aere natum.

At neque dedecorant tua de se iudicia atque
munera, quae multa dantis cum laude tulerunt,
dilecti tibi Vergilius Variusque poetae
nec magis expressi vultus per aenea signa
quam per vatis opus mores animique virorum
clarorum apparent. nec sermones ego mallem
repentis per humum quam res componere gestas
terrarumque situs et flumina dicere et arces

So finely drawn, so elegantly spun out;
And when we hope that the very minute you hear
That we are poets you will summon us
Into your presence, command us to write poems,
And forbid us to be poor.
                              But it would be
Very much worth your while to know exactly
Whom you're choosing to tend the temple of
Your deeds of peace and war. It's not a task
To be entrusted to an unworthy poet.
Alexander the Great was greatly pleased to be pleased
With old Choerilus and filled his pockets
With lots of royal cash, as a reward
For his misbegotten badly written verses.
A page can be spoiled by ink not handled rightly;
Great deeds can be blurred and smudged by a bad poem.
That very same king who paid so much for such
A ridiculous poem put out an edict forbidding
Anyone but Apelles to paint his portrait
And anyone but Lysippus to work in bronze
To celebrate the face of Alexander.
If you judged his judgment of books and poetic talent
By the same high standards he used about works of art,
You'd conclude that Alexander in this regard
Was as stupid as if he'd been born in Boeotia.
But Varius and Virgil, whom you love,
Do not dishonor your generosity.
In the poetry they write, the character
And mind of the virtuous famous man is shown
As clearly as his features are shown in bronze.

Rather than poetry of the sort I write
That keeps itself so close to the level ground,
I'd much prefer to be able to be the teller
Of tales of heroic deeds, of barbarous kingdoms,
Far-off lands and rivers, forts built high
In mountain fastnesses, the Parthians
Transfixed by the power of dread of Caesar's might;

montibus impositas et barbara regna tuisque
auspiciis totum confecta duella per orbem
claustraque custodem pacis cohibentia Ianum
et formidatam Parthis te principe Romam,
si quantum cuperem possem quoque. sed neque parvum
carmen maiestas recipit tua nec meus audet
rem temptare pudor quam vires ferre recusent.
sedulitas autem, stulte quem diligit, urget,
praecipue cum se numeris commendat et arte;
discit enim citius meminitque libentius illud
quod quis deridet quam quod probat et veneratur.
nil moror officium quod me gravat, ac neque ficto
in peius vultu proponi cereus usquam
nec prave factis decorari versibus opto,
ne rubeam pingui donatus munere et una
cum scriptore meo, capsa porrectus operta,
deferar in vicum vendentem tus et odores
et piper et quidquid chartis amicitur ineptis.

And all wars finally brought to an end, so that
The Gate of guardian Janus can be closed.
I wish I had the power to do what I wish.
But the grandeur of your deeds is out of scale
For such poetry as mine; and my self-knowledge
Keeps me from trying for more than I have the strength for.
That ardor is ridiculous that goes
Beyond its limits, badgering what it loves,
Especially if the badgering's metrical—
And writers of foolish poems often find
They're vividly and scornfully remembered.

I know that I myself wouldn't relish being
Acclaimed in some wrongheaded panegyric
Or having my face, misshapen, portrayed in wax.
This fatuous praise would make me blush with shame,
As, with my praiser, the two of us together
Are carried off, stretched out in a closed casket,
Down to the street where cheap perfume is sold,
Incense, pepper, spices, and all sorts of other
Odoriferous things wrapped up in old waste paper.

Flore, bono claroque fidelis amice Neroni,
si quis forte velit puerum tibi vendere natum
Tibure vel Gabiis et tecum sic agat: 'hic et
candidus et talos a vertice pulcher ad imos
fiet eritque tuus nummorum milibus octo,
verna ministeriis ad nutus aptus erilis,
litterulis Graecis imbutus, idoneus arti
cuilibet; argilla quidvis imitaberis uda.
quin etiam canet, indoctum sed dulce bibenti.
multa fidem promissa levant, ubi plenius aequo
laudat venalis qui vult extrudere merces:
res urget me nulla; meo sum pauper in aere.
nemo hoc mangonum faceret tibi; non temere a me
quivis ferret idem. semel hic cessavit et, ut fit,
in scalis latuit metuens pendentis habenae.
des nummos, excepta nihil te si fuga laedit:'
ille ferat pretium poenae securus, opinor.
prudens emisti vitiosum; dicta tibi est lex:
insequeris tamen hunc et lite moraris iniqua?
dixi me pigrum proficiscenti tibi, dixi
talibus officiis prope mancum, ne mea saevus
iurgares ad te quod epistula nulla rediret.
quid tum profeci, mecum facientia iura
si tamen attemptas?

ii.2

TO JULIUS FLORUS

Florus, dear friend, suppose somebody offered
To sell you a slave, and made the following sales pitch:
"A good-looking boy; the asking price 8,000;
Born in Italy; very willing and able;
He reads a little Greek; a very quick learner;
He's malleable, you can make of him what you will;
At drink time he can sing you a song or two,
Pleasingly if somewhat artlessly.
Believe you me, when a salesman like me is under
Pressure to make a sale and anxiously makes
Too many promises, why then of course he loses
The customer's trust. But *I'm* under no such pressure.
I have no debts. None of the other dealers
Is able to make you such an offer as this,
Nor would I make it to just anyone.
Something I ought to tell you: there was one time
When the boy ran off, in a truant way, and hid
Under the stairs, because he was scared of a whipping.
If you're not bothered by this peccadillo
I've told you about, give me the price I ask."

I think the salesman who handled the sale this way
Would make the sale and get his price, without worry.
If the customer had bought with his eyes open,
He'd know what the boy had done. If it happened again,
Wouldn't it be unjust to sue the salesman?
I told you when you were leaving, how lazy I am,
A couch potato. I told you so you wouldn't
Scold me for never answering your letters.

Quereris super hoc etiam quod
exspectata tibi non mittam carmina mendax.
Luculli miles collecta viatica multis
aerumnis, lassus dum noctu stertit, ad assem
perdiderat. post hoc vehemens lupus, et sibi et hosti
iratus pariter, ieiunis dentibus acer,
praesidium regale loco deiecit, ut aiunt,
summe munito et multarum divite rerum.
clarus ob id factum donis ornatur honestis,
accipit et bis dena super sestertia nummum.
forte sub hoc tempus castellum evertere praetor
nescio quod cupiens, hortari coepit eundem
verbis quae timido quoque possent addere mentem:
'i, bone, quo virtus tua te vocat, i pede fausto,
grandia laturus meritorum praemia. quid stas?'
post haec ille catus, quantumvis rusticus, 'ibit,
ibit eo quo vis qui zonam perdidit' inquit.

Romae nutriri mihi contigit atque doceri
iratus Grais quantum nocuisset Achilles.
adiecere bonae paulo plus artis Athenae,
scilicet ut vellem curvo dinoscere rectum
atque inter silvas Academi quaerere verum.
dura sed emovere loco me tempora grato
civilisque rudem belli tulit aestus in arma
Caesaris Augusti non responsura lacertis.
unde simul primum me dimisere Philippi,
decisis humilem pennis inopemque paterni
et Laris et fundi paupertas impulit audax
ut versus facerem; sed quod non desit habentem
quae poterunt umquam satis expurgare cicutae,
ni melius dormire putem quam scribere versus?

What was the point of telling you this if you
Still scold me, not only about the letters but
About the unsent poems I promised to send.

Once upon a time in Lucullus's army
There was a soldier who by working hard
Had saved a lot of money, but then, one night,
All of it was stolen. Gnashing his teeth
Like a starving wolf, furious at himself
And furious at whoever it was who stole it,
He single-handedly drove out a royal
Garrison from a fortified position
Where there was stored an awful lot of riches.
Glory he won and more than 20,000
Sesterces in reward for this exploit.
A short time afterwards his captain wanted
To attack another fort, and, using terms
That might have stirred up courage in the heart
Of even the timidest of men, he said,
"Go where your valor tells you to go, stout heart!
Good fortune come to you! Win the rewards
Your deeds deserve!—Why are you standing still?"
To which the rustic fellow said, "Why don't you
Tell it to somebody who's just lost his money."

I got my schooling in Rome and learned about
How bad Achilles' anger was for the Greeks,
And then of course I went on to Athens to study
Eagerly under those Academic trees
The nature of truth and how to tell crooked from straight.
And then the hard times came, and I was taken,
A raw recruit, away from that pleasant grove
And swept by the tide of war onto the field,
Among the others fighting with weapons useless
Against the powerful arms of Caesar Augustus.
Philippi happened and so I was discharged,
But my wings were clipped, and I was stripped of money
And stripped of my father's property. And so

Singula de nobis anni praedantur euntes.
eripuere iocos, Venerem, convivia, ludum,
tendunt extorquere poemata. quid faciam vis?

Denique non omnes eadem mirantur amantque:
carmine tu gaudes, hic delectatur iambis,
ille Bioneis sermonibus et sale nigro.
tres mihi convivae prope dissentire videntur,
poscentes vario multum diversa palato.
quid dem? quid non dem? renuis tu quod iubet alter;
quod petis, id sane est invisum acidumque duobus.

Praeter cetera me Romaene poemata censes
scribere posse inter tot curas totque labores?
hic sponsum vocat, hic auditum scripta relictis
omnibus officiis; cubat hic in colle Quirini,
hic extremo in Aventino, visendus uterque;
intervalla vides haud sane commoda. 'verum
purae sunt plateae, nihil ut meditantibus obstet.'
festinat calidus mulis gerulisque redemptor,
torquet nunc lapidem, nunc ingens machina tignum,
tristia robustis luctantur funera plaustris,
hac rabiosa fugit canis, hac lutulenta ruit sus:

It was because of poverty that I
Was forced to write my verses. But now that I'm
Pretty well off, what drug do you think I'd take
To make me think it better to write than sleep?

The years as they go by take everything with them,
One thing after another; they've taken away
Laughter, and revelry, and love from me, and now
They want to take poetry. What can I do?
Not everybody's the same in matters of taste.
You like my songs; another likes my epodes;
Another of you likes my caustic satires.
It seems to me it's as if three guests for dinner
Had likes and dislikes in food that were all at odds.
So what should I serve up? What should I not?
For you'd send back to the kitchen what one of them ordered,
And what you like disgusts the other two.

And anyway, what makes you think that I
Can write in Rome, with all I have to do there?
First this one wants a letter of introduction;
Then that one wants me to put aside everything
And listen to what he's written only this morning;
Then somebody else, who lives on the Quirinal,
Is sick in bed, and so is somebody else,
Who lives way off on the back of the Aventine,
And I'm supposed to sickroom visit both.
"Well, but the streets are quiet, so you'll be able
To think about your poems on your way over."
Oh, sure. Tell me about it. First there'll be
A contractor with his gear and all his workmen,
And then a giant crane in the way, first hoisting
A great huge stone and then a great huge log,
And then here comes a funeral procession
Jostling its way along through all the traffic
Of great huge rattling wagons, and all of a sudden
A mad dog runs by one way through the street
And a filthy runaway pig the other way.

i nunc et versus tecum meditare canoros!
scriptorum chorus omnis amat nemus et fugit urbem,
rite cliens Bacchi somno gaudentis et umbra:
tu me inter strepitus nocturnos atque diurnos
vis canere et contracta sequi vestigia vatum?
ingenium sibi quod vacuas desumpsit Athenas
et studiis annos septem dedit insenuitque
libris et curis, statua taciturnius exit
plerumque et risu populum quatit: hic ego rerum
fluctibus in mediis et tempestatibus urbis
verba lyrae motura sonum conectere digner?

Frater erat Romae consulti rhetor, ut alter
alterius sermone meros audiret honores,
Gracchus ut hic illi, foret huic ut Mucius ille.
qui minus argutos vexat furor iste poetas?
carmina compono, hic elegos. 'mirabile visu
caelatumque novem Musis opus!' aspice primum
quanto cum fastu, quanto molimine circum-
spectemus vacuam Romanis vatibus aedem!
mox etiam, si forte vacas, sequere et procul audi
quid ferat et quare sibi nectat uterque coronam.
caedimur et totidem plagis consumimus hostem
lento Samnites ad lumina prima duello.
discedo Alcaeus puncto illius: ille meo quis?
quis nisi Callimachus? si plus apposcere visus,
fit Mimnermus et optivo cognomine crescit.
multa fero, ut placem genus irritabile vatum,
cum scribo et supplex populi suffragia capto;
idem, finitis studiis et mente recepta,
obturem patulas impune legentibus auris.

"Work on writing sonorous verses en route"?
The choir of poets loves groves and hates the city,
Faithful to Bacchus, who loves to sleep in the shade.
Do you really want me to follow the path of art
Amid all the noise that goes on all day and all night?
An artist who's made the choice to live in Athens,
A quiet place like that, even there, when he
Comes out of his study and walks about the town,
He's tongue-tied as a statue, an object of laughter.
In Rome, in the social hubbub, do you suppose
That I'd be able to put together the words
That would awaken the music of the lyre?

There were two brothers in Rome, one was a lawyer,
The other an orator, and all day long
All you could hear were the praises of each for the other.
If one of them was a Gracchus to the other,
The other one was a Mucius to his brother.
It's just like that with our nest of singing bards.
I write an ode; my friend an elegy:
"Oh, marvelous! You're blessed by all nine Muses!"
If you could see with what complacency
We stand in that room in the Library of Apollo
Companionably eyeing the medallions
Of famous dead authors there, and then if you
Drew near and listened to how we talk to each other,
You'd find out how our ivy crowns get woven.
Like Samnite fighters in an endless battle
We bash each other with compliments as we go at it.
He says to me, "You're exactly like Alcaeus!"
And according to me, he is?—"Callimachus."
And if he seems to need more, then he's "Mimnermus,"
And so he gets the title that he wants.
I used to go out of my way to soothe the nerves
Of anxious touchy writers, when I myself
Was writing and touchy and anxiously seeking approval,
But now that that's all over, now that I'm back
In my right mind, I'd gladly stop up my ears
When anyone threatens to read me what he's just written.

Ridentur mala qui componunt carmina; verum
gaudent scribentes et se venerantur et ultro,
si taceas, laudant quidquid scripsere beati.
at qui legitimum cupiet fecisse poema,
cum tabulis animum censoris sumet honesti;
audebit, quaecumque parum splendoris habebunt
et sine pondere erunt et honore indigna fruentur,
verba movere loco, quamvis invita recedant
et versentur adhuc intra penetralia Vestae.
obscurata diu populo bonus eruet atque
proferet in lucem speciosa vocabula rerum,
quae priscis memorata Catonibus atque Cethegis
nunc situs informis premit et deserta vetustas;
asciscet nova, quae genitor produxerit usus.
vehemens et liquidus puroque simillimus amni
fundet opes Latiumque beabit divite lingua.
luxuriantia compescet, nimis aspera sano
levabit cultu, virtute carentia tollet.
ludentis speciem dabit et torquebitur, ut qui
nunc Satyrum, nunc agrestem Cyclopa movetur.

Praetulerim scriptor delirus inersque videri,
dum mea delectent mala me vel denique fallant,
quam sapere et ringi. fuit haud ignobilis Argis,
qui se credebat miros audire tragoedos

People who write bad poetry are a joke,
But writing makes them happy and it makes them
Happily reverential of themselves.
If they hear no praise from you, what do they care?
Deaf to your silence they'll praise themselves, serenely.
But he who desires to write a legitimate poem
Will be an honest critic of what he does.
He won't be afraid, if some expression doesn't
Seem right, if it lacks the appropriate weight or luster,
Or if it's wrong for the tone of the passage it's part of,
To take it away, although it's reluctant to go
And struggles to keep the place it felt enshrined in.
He'll dig up obscure old words such as Cato used,
Or Cethegus used, and bring them back, from where
They'd languished in the dark of the long ago,
Into the light of day, alive with meaning.
He'll be willing to use new words in poetry,
Made valid by their valid use by men
Going about their daily work or play.
Steady, flowing, pure, just as a river
Is steady, flowing, and pure, he will pour forth
Power, and bless his country with a rich language.
He'll prune back whatever is overgrown, smooth out
Whatever is rough, get rid of whatever weakness
Inhibits power; he'll make it look like child's play,
Although, in fact, he tortures himself to do so;
His dancing moves with grace, like a satyr, now,
And now the way an oafish Cyclops moves.

I think I'd just as soon be thought to be
A silly and incompetent hack, so long
As I was perfectly happy with my faults
Or perfectly unaware of them, rather than be
Grinding my teeth to endure my own self-knowledge.
Once there was at Argos a well-regarded
Citizen whose mind was taken over
By the fantasy that he was sitting alone,
A privileged audience of one, in a theater,

in vacuo laetus sessor plausorque theatro;
cetera qui vitae servaret munia recto
more, bonus sane vicinus, amabilis hospes,
comis in uxorem, posset qui ignoscere servis
et signo laeso non insanire lagoenae,
posset qui rupem et puteum vitare patentem.
hic ubi cognatorum opibus curisque refectus
expulit elleboro morbum bilemque meraco
et redit ad sese, 'pol me occidistis, amici,
non servastis' ait, 'cui sic extorta voluptas
et demptus per vim mentis gratissimus error.'

Nimirum sapere est abiectis utile nugis
et tempestivum pueris concedere ludum,
ac non verba sequi fidibus modulanda Latinis,
sed verae numerosque modosque ediscere vitae.
quocirca mecum loquor haec tacitusque recordor:
si tibi nulla sitim finiret copia lymphae,
narrares medicis: quod quanto plura parasti,
tanto plura cupis, nulline faterier audes?
si vulnus tibi monstrata radice vel herba
non fieret levius, fugeres radice vel herba
proficiente nihil curarier. audieras, cui
rem di donarent, illi decedere pravam
stultitiam: et cum sis nihilo sapientior ex quo
plenior es, tamen uteris monitoribus isdem?

Enthusiastically applauding as he listened
To a marvelous company of tragic actors
Performing just for him. This citizen
In every other way was entirely normal:
He never had any trouble with the neighbors;
He was a genial host, and kind to his wife;
If one of his servants happened to break a jar,
He didn't go crazy, he wasn't that kind of master.
In short, this man was the sort of person who wasn't
Likely to fall down a well or over a cliff.
His relatives worried about his fantasy
And got him cured with a dose of hellebore,
But when he was cured and back in his senses he told them:
"You think you've cured me but actually you've killed me.
The illusion you took away was what I lived on."

Certainly it's right to put away
All childish things and leave to children such games
As trying to find exactly the proper words
To calibrate to the cadences and meter
Of the Latin lyre, and right to study instead
The cadences and meter of living right.
That's why, over and over, I find myself
Thinking about things in the following ways:
Suppose you had a thirst nothing would quench;
The more water you drank, the more you wanted.
You'd go to a doctor. And if the richer you get,
The richer you need to be, isn't there someone
You need to consult? Suppose you had a sore
And the herbs the doctor prescribed weren't able to cure it,
Wouldn't you give up using the herbs he prescribed?
Maybe somebody told you that the richer
You got to be with possessions the gods had given,
The freer you'd be from being possessed by folly;
Now that you're richer, you know, you're not a bit wiser.
Maybe it's time to listen to somebody else.
If money could give you wisdom and free you from folly
And free you from anxiety, then surely

at si divitiae prudentem reddere possent,
si cupidum timidumque minus te, nempe ruberes,
viveret in terris te si quis avarior uno.

Si proprium est quod quis libra mercatus et aere est,
quaedam, si credis consultis, mancipat usus.
qui te pascit ager tuus est et vilicus Orbi,
cum segetes occat tibi mox frumenta daturas,
te dominum sentit. das nummos, accipis uvam,
pullos, ova, cadum temeti: nempe modo isto
paulatim mercaris agrum, fortasse trecentis
aut etiam supra nummorum milibus emptum.
quid refert, vivas numerato nuper an olim?
emptor Aricini quondam Veientis et arvi
emptum cenat holus, quamvis aliter putat, emptis
sub noctem gelidam lignis calefactat aenum;
sed vocat usque suum qua populus assita certis
limitibus vicina refringit iurgia, tamquam
sit proprium quidquam puncto quod mobilis horae
nunc prece, nunc pretio, nunc vi, nunc morte suprema
permutet dominos et cedat in altera iura.

Sic quia perpetuus nulli datur usus et heres
heredem alternis velut unda supervenit undam,
quid vici prosunt aut horrea, quidve Calabris
saltibus adiecti Lucani, si metit Orcus
grandia cum parvis, non exorabilis auro?

You'd be abashed if there was anyone
Anywhere in the world more greedy than you.

Of course it's true that if you've signed the deeds
And paid a lot of money, then you're the owner
Of what you've paid and signed for. But if you listen
To what they say who are learned in the law,
Use is a kind of ownership as well.
In a sense you're the owner of any farm that feeds you;
You're the master of the farmer who plows the land,
Preparing it for the corn you're going to buy.
You pay some money, and you own some eggs,
A chicken, some grapes, maybe some wine, and so,
Little by little you're buying the farm that someone
Once paid 300,000 sesterces or more for.
What difference whether the payment was now or then?
The man who's bought a farm out at Aricia
Has only bought, no matter what he thinks,
The salad for his dinner, the logs for the fire
To heat the kettle on, of a chilly evening.
His view of the matter is of course that he owns
The whole kit and caboodle, over to where
The poplars are planted to mark the boundary clearly,
To head off possible neighborly disputes.
Imagine somebody thinking he's the owner,
When what he thinks he owns so easily passes
Into the hands of somebody else, say by
Foreclosure or by eminent domain,
Or, if no other way, at the last, by death.
So if nobody has the use of anything
In perpetuity, and therefore if
Heir follows heir as one wave follows another,
What is the use of storehouses full of grain
From your vast estate, or vast extents of forests
In Lucania, and others in Calabria,
If Death, who can't be tempted by your money,
Gathers the rich man in along with the poor?
Jewels, marble, ivory, paintings, beautiful Tuscan

gemmas, marmor, ebur, Tyrrhena sigilla, tabellas,
argentum, vestis Gaetulo murice tinctas
sunt qui non habeant, est qui non curat habere.
cur alter fratrum cessare et ludere et ungui
praeferat Herodis palmetis pinguibus, alter
dives et importunus ad umbram lucis ab ortu
silvestrem flammis et ferro mitiget agrum,
scit Genius, natale comes qui temperat astrum,
naturae deus humanae mortalis in unum
quodque caput, vultu mutabilis, albus et ater.

Utar et ex modico quantum res poscet acervo
tollam, nec metuam quid de me iudicet heres,
quod non plura datis invenerit; et tamen idem
scire volam quantum simplex hilarisque nepoti
discrepet et quantum discordet parcus avaro.
distat enim spargas tua prodigus an neque sumptum
invitus facias neque plura parare labores,
ac potius, puer ut festis Quinquatribus olim,
exiguo gratoque fruatis tempore raptim.
pauperies immunda domus procul absit ego utrum
nave ferar magna an parva, ferar unus et idem.

Pottery, silver, Gaetulian robes dyed purple—
Many there are who'd love to have all of these things.
There are some who don't care about them in the least.
Why one twin brother lives for nothing but pleasure,
And loves to fool around even more than Herod
Loves his abundant gardens of date-trees, while
The other twin brother works from morning to night
Improving his farm, ploughing and clearing the lands,
Pruning and planting, working his ass off, only
The Genius knows, the personal god who knows
And controls the birth star of every person
There is in the world. (Your personal god is the god
Who dies in a sense when your own breath gives out,
And yet lives on, after you die, to be
The personal god of somebody other than you;
Your personal god, whose countenance changes as
He looks at you, smiling sometimes, sometimes not.)

I'll do the best I can with what I have,
And I'm not going to worry about whatever
My heir might think because I've left so little.
But at the same time I want to be sure I know
The difference there is between the spendthrift and
The man who's openhearted and generous,
And also the difference there is between the man
Who's prudent because he knows the value of things
And the miser who simply can't let anything go.
There *is* a distinction between just wantonly
Throwing your money away in a prodigal fashion
And being perfectly willing to spend and not
Unduly concerned with holding on to it all,
Seizing the chance for pleasure when it comes,
Like a schoolboy let out of school at holiday time.
Keep direst poverty far away from me;
But other than that, whether the ship be large
Or be it small that I'm a passenger on,
I'm still the same passenger, always one and the same,
Not always sped full sail by a favoring wind

non agimur tumidis velis Aquilone secundo;
non tamen adversis aetatem ducimus Austris:
viribus, ingenio, specie, virtute, loco, re
extremi primorum, extremis usque priores.

Non es avarus? abi. quid? cetera iam simul isto
cum vitio fugere? caret tibi pectus inani
ambitione? caret mortis formidine et ira?
somnia, terrores magicos, miracula, sagas,
nocturnos lemures portentaque Thessala rides?
natalis grate numeras? ignoscis amicis?
lenior et melior fis accedente senecta?
quid te exempta levat spinis de pluribus una?
vivere si recte nescis, decede peritis.
lusisti satis, edisti satis atque bibisti.
tempus abire tibi est, ne potum largius aequo
rideat et pulset lasciva decentius aetas.

And yet not always laboring through a storm,
Always more or less what I was before,
In my person and place in life somewhere behind
Those who are first, somewhere ahead of the last.

You're not avaricious? Fine. But, tell me, did
All other frailties go away when that did?
Are you free in your heart from hungry ambition, say?
Are you scared to death by the very thought of death?
Are you able to laugh at dreams, or the spooks of magic?
At wizards? Ghosts? Things that go whoosh in the night?
Thessalian wizards' omens? Do you count with relief
Every new birthday you've managed to make it through?
Do you always forgive the faults you see in your friends?
Are you getting any better as you get older?
Are you any kinder than you used to be?
What have you gained if you've plucked out just one thorn,
When you've got so many others in your foot?
If you haven't learned yet how to live right, well, then,
Get out of the way of others who might learn better.
You've played enough, you've eaten and drunk enough;
Maybe it's time to say goodbye, before
You've had too much to drink and get made fun of
And elbowed out by younger people who know
Better than you do how to have fun at the party.

ARS POETICA

Humano capiti cervicem pictor equinam
iungere si velit et varias inducere plumas
undique collatis membris, ut turpiter atrum
desinat in piscem mulier formosa superne,
spectatum admissi risum teneatis, amici?
credite, Pisones, isti tabulae fore librum
persimilem cuius, velut aegri somnia, vanae
fingentur species, ut nec pes nec caput uni
reddatur formae. 'pictoribus atque poetis
quidlibet audendi semper fuit aequa potestas.'
scimus, et hanc veniam petimusque damusque vicissim;
sed non ut placidis coeant immitia, non ut
serpentes avibus geminentur, tigribus agni.

Inceptis gravibus plerumque et magna professis
purpureus, late qui splendeat, unus et alter
assuitur pannus, cum lucus et ara Dianae
et properantis aquae per amoenos ambitus agros,
aut flumen Rhenum aut pluvius describitur arcus.

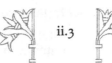

ii.3

Suppose some painter had the bright idea
Of sticking a human head on a horse's neck
And covering human nether limbs up with
Assorted feathers so that a beautiful
Woman uptop was an ugly fish below,
And you were invited in to take a look,
How could you possibly manage to keep a straight face?
Dear Pisos, dear friends, a poem's exactly like
Such pictures as those, when the poet's fantasies
Are like a sick man's raving dreams in which
You can't tell head from foot nor what it is
That they're attached to. "Poets and painters," you say,
"Have the right to do whatever they dare to do."
Well, yes. We poets claim that right for ourselves
And recognize that other artists have it.
But it doesn't go so far as mixing up
Savage and civilized, mating tigers and lambs,
Or having serpents get it on with birds.
There are works that begin in genuine nobleness
And therefore make large genuine promises
Yet sometimes they're stuck about with shining purple
Patches that catch the eye: for example, a pause
To tell you all about Diana's grove,
Or "the stream that winds yet hastens through the fields,"
Or to have you admire the far-off scenic Rhine
Or the rainbow you can see when the storm is over.
There are places for things like these, but often not
In the places where they occur. If what you know
Is how to draw the picture of a cypress,

sed nunc non erat his locus. et fortasse cupressum
scis simulare: quid hoc, si fractis enatat exspes
navibus aere dato qui pingitur? amphora coepit
institui: currente rota cur urceus exit?
denique sit quidvis, simplex dumtaxat et unum.

Maxima pars vatum, pater et iuvenes patre digni,
decipimur specie recti. brevis esse laboro,
obscurus fio; sectantem levia nervi
deficiunt animique; professus grandia turget;
serpit humi tutus nimium timidusque procellae.
qui variare cupit rem prodigialiter unam,
delphinum silvis appingit, fluctibus aprum:
in vitium ducit culpae fuga, si caret arte.
Aemilium circa Ludum faber unus et unguis
exprimet et mollis imitabitur aere capillos,
infelix operis summa, quia ponere totum
nesciet. hunc ego me, si quid componere curem,
non magis esse velim quam naso vivere pravo,
spectandum nigris oculis nigroque capillo.

Sumite materiam vestris, qui scribitis, aequam
viribus et versate diu quid ferre recusent,
quid valeant umeri; cui lecta pudenter erit res,
nec facundia deseret hunc nec lucidus ordo.

That's not much use if what you're paid to do
Is to paint the picture of a panicked sailor
Swimming away from the sinking wreck of his ship.
Why does what was supposed to turn out to be
A wine jar, when the job began, turn out,
When the pottery wheel stops turning, to be a jug?
In short, whatever the work is supposed to be,
Let it be true to itself, essentially simple.

Father and worthy sons, we poets often
Know what we're aiming at, and often we miss.
I try my best to be terse, and I'm obscure;
I try for mellifluous smoothness, smooth as can be,
And the line comes out as spineless as a worm;
One poet, aiming for grandeur, booms and blusters;
Another one, scared, creeps his way under the storm;
And another, desiring to vary his single theme
In wonderful ways, produces not wonders but monsters—
Dolphins up in the trees, pigs in the ocean.
If you don't know what you're doing you can go wrong
Just out of trying to do your best to do right.
Down near the Aemilian School there's a craftsman's shop
Where he's very good at imitating in bronze
Things like toenails, say, or wavy hair,
But it turns out badly because in fact he isn't
Any good at all at doing the whole body.
If I wanted to write a poem, I'd no more want
To be like him than if I were happy to live with
My nose all crooked and funny, just because
I was praised for my shining dark eyes and lustrous hair.

Aspiring writer, be sure to be careful to pick
Material that you're strong enough to handle;
Give careful consideration to the question
Of what your shoulders can carry and what they can't.
The man who does this will find he doesn't have trouble
Thinking of what to say and in what order.
Order's important: the virtue and beauty of some
Long-promised poem, unless I'm mistaken, often

Ordinis haec virtus erit et Venus, aut ego fallor,
ut iam nunc dicat iam nunc debentia dici,
pleraque differat et praesens in tempus omittat.

Hoc amet, hoc spernat promissi carminis auctor.
in verbis etiam tenuis cautusque serendis
dixeris egregie, notum si callida verbum
reddiderit iunctura novum. si forte necesse est
indiciis monstrare recentibus abdita rerum,
fingere cinctutis non exaudita Cethegis
continget dabiturque licentia sumpta pudenter;
et nova fictaque nuper habebunt verba fidem si
Graeco fonte cadent, parce detorta. quid autem
Caecilio Plautoque dabit Romanus ademptum
Vergilio Varioque? ego cur, acquirere pauca
si possum, invideor, cum lingua Catonis et Enni
sermonem patrium ditaverit et nova rerum
nomina protulerit? licuit semperque licebit
signatum praesente nota procudere nummum.
ut silvae foliis privos mutantur in annos,
prima cadunt * * * * * * * * *
* * * * * ita verborum vetus interit aetas
et iuvenum ritu florent modo nata vigentque.
debemur morti nos nostraque; sive receptus
terra Neptunus classis Aquilonibus arcet,
regis opus, sterilisve diu palus aptaque remis
vicinas urbis alit et grave sentit aratrum,
seu cursum mutavit iniquum frugibus amnis
doctus iter melius: mortalia facta peribunt,
nedum sermonum stet honos et gratia vivax.

Depends on the author having judiciously chosen
To say the thing that ought to be said right now,
And keeping other things back for later on,
Favoring one thing over against another.

And furthermore, if you're shrewd about how to do it,
And do it very carefully, you can work it
So that the context makes a word that's worn
From being too familiar seem brand-new;
And if it comes about that you have to invent
New words because your subject's so abstract
Or recondite, you can invent new words
The Cethegi in their loincloths never heard of,
And you'll get away with it, as long as you do it
Circumspectly—you can get by with words
Recently coined if you get them from the Greek,
And if you don't attempt to *over*do it.
Why on earth should Caecilius and Plautus
Be allowed to do what Virgil and Varius aren't?
And why should I be sneered at if I try
To add my little bit, when Ennius and Cato
Gave us new names for things, and doing so made
Our language by what they did so much the richer?
It's always been allowed, and always will be,
To introduce new words, fresh from the mint.
Just as in forests in the changing year
New leaves come in and the oldest drop away,
So is it with words: the old ones die away
And the new ones bloom and prosper in their time.
We and all that we do are bound to die—
The royal work that welcomes in the sea,
Sheltering fleets from storms in man-made bays;
The useless swamp, once fit for nothing but oars,
Now fit for the plow, and nourishing its towns;
The river once the ruiner of fields
Now taught the art of going its harmless way—
All things that mortals do and build are mortal;
How mortal then the glories of our speech.
Words that have fallen away may rise again;

multa renascentur quae iam cecidere, cadentque
quae nunc sunt in honore vocabula, si volet usus,
quem penes arbitrium est et ius et norma loquendi.

Res gestae regumque ducumque et tristia bella
quo scribi possent numero, monstravit Homerus.
versibus impariter iunctis querimonia primum,
post etiam inclusa est voti sententia compos;
quis tamen exiguos elegos emiserit auctor,
grammatici certant et adhuc sub iudice lis est.
Archilochum proprio rabies armavit iambo;
hunc socci cepere pedem grandesque cothurni
alternis aptum sermonibus et populalis
vincentem strepitus et natum rebus agendis.
Musa dedit fidibus divos puerosque deorum
et pugilem victorem et equum certamine primum
et iuvenum curas et libera vina referre.
descriptas servare vices operumque colores
cur ego si nequeo ignoroque poeta salutor?
cur nescire pudens prave quam discere malo?
versibus exponi tragicis res comica non vult;

Words now in honor may fall, if Use, which is
The governor of our language, should decide.

Homer first showed us how the verse should move
That tells the deeds of kings and sorrows of war.
Lines paired unequally, as spoken brokenhearted,
Perhaps were first a vehicle of grief,
Lamenting one who died, and after that became
A vehicle of thanks for health restored
After a votive offering; it's not entirely clear,
The scholarly jury is out, concerning how
The verse called elegiac came into being and who
Was the first poet who wrote it, and for what reason.

Raging Archilocus used iambic meter
To be his rage's weapon; and it was also
Appropriate for the theater as well,
For comic sock and tragic buskin both,
Because its urgent alternating rhythm
Propels the energies of the dialogue
And drives the action forward and wins out over
The coughs and whispers of the customers.

To the cadences of the lyre the Muse gave stories
Of gods and of their children, and stories of how
The boxer won his victory in the ring
And the racehorse came in first at the hippodrome,
And stories of lovers' cares, and the joys of wine.

If I didn't know how these ways of writing differ
In what they are suited for, and if I didn't
Act on what I knew, tell me, would I
Have any right to be credited as a poet?
Why should I be ashamed of having knowledge?
Comedy oughtn't to want to be set out
In measures appropriate for tragedy;
The terrible family meal Thyestes ate
Ought not to be told about in an everyday manner

indignatur item privatis ac prope socco
dignis carminibus narrari cena Thyestae.
singula quaeque locum teneant sortita decentem.
interdum tamen et vocem comoedia tollit
iratusque Chremes tumido delitigat ore
et tragicus plerumque dolet sermone pedestri
Telephus et Peleus, cum pauper et exsul uterque
proicit ampullas et sesquipedalia verba,
si curat cor spectantis tetigisse querela.

Non satis est pulchra esse poemata; dulcia sunto,
et quocumque volent animum auditoris agunto.
ut ridentibus arrident, ita flentibus afflent
humani vultus: si vis me flere, dolendum est
primum ipsi tibi. tum tua me infortunia laedent,
Telephe vel Peleu; male si mandata loqueris,
aut dormitabo aut ridebo. tristia maestum
vultum verba decent, iratum plena minarum,
ludentem lasciva, severum seria dictu.
format enim Natura prius nos intus ad omnem
fortunarum habitum; iuvat aut impellit ad iram
aut ad humum maerore gravi deducit et angit;
post effert animi motus interprete lingua.
si dicentis erunt fortunis absona dicta,
Romani tollent equites peditesque cachinnum.
intererit multum divusne loquatur an heros,
maturusne senex an adhuc florente iuventa
fervidus, et matrona potens an sedula nutrix,
mercatorne vagus cultorne virentis agelli,
Colchus an Assyrius, Thebis nutritus an Argis.

Appropriate on the stage for comedy.
Let every genre keep to its proper style.
There are times, to be sure, when comedy raises its voice
And irate roaring Chremes berates his son;
And sometimes it's the case, in tragedy,
When Peleus or Telephus is grieving,
In poverty, in exile, he must give up
His vaunting high heroic words and use
Instead of these the language of common speech,
In order to touch the hearts of those who listen.
Sheer abstract beauty isn't enough in a poem;
Its language must so persuade the listener
And act upon his soul that he'll respond
As the poem intends. Men smile if the language smiles;
They weep if the language truly weeps. If you
Desire to hear me weep, you must truly grieve,
O Peleus or Telephus, and I'll
Grieve as if I suffered your cause of grief;
But if your words don't suit your circumstance,
Then I may laugh at them—or fall asleep.
The countenance of sorrow requires a deeply
Expressive language of sorrow; anger should shake
And reverberate with its rage; delight in the joke
Should play and delight in the words of the way it's told;
Sobriety move to the sound of its own grave music.
For Nature has made us such that we're in a sense
Ready for all that happens, expressive creatures;
She gives us cause for joy, and cause for sorrow,
She humbles us down to the ground, oppressed with trouble,
And she gives us the tongue with which to tell how it is.

If the actor's words don't fit his circumstance,
The audience, high and low, will burst out laughing.
It makes a difference who it is who's speaking,
If he's a god, or a hero, a seasoned old man,
A youth in the flower of youth, a rich Roman matron,
A busy old nurse, a wandering merchant, a farmer,
An Assyrian, Colchian, Argive or a Theban.

Aut famam sequere aut sibi convenientia finge.
scriptor honoratum si forte reponis Achillem,
impiger, iracundus, inexorabilis, acer
iura neget sibi nata, nihil non arroget armis.
sit Medea ferox invictaque, flebilis Ino,
perfidus Ixion, Io vaga, tristis Orestes.
si quid inexpertum scaenae committis et audes
personam formare novam, servetur ad imum
qualis ab incepto processerit et sibi constet.
difficile est proprie communia dicere, tuque
rectius Iliacum carmen diducis in actus
quam si proferres ignota indictaque primus.
publica materies privati iuris erit, si
non circa vilem patulumque moraberis orbem,
nec verbo verbum curabis reddere fidus
interpres, nec desilies imitator in artum,
unde pedem proferre pudor vetet aut operis lex.

Nec sic incipies ut scriptor cyclicus olim:
'fortunam Priami cantabo et nobile bellum.'
quid dignum tanto feret hic promissor hiatu?
parturient montes, nascetur ridiculus mus.
quanto rectius hic qui nil molitur inepte!
'dic mihi, Musa, virum, captae post tempora Troiae
qui mores hominum multorum vidit et urbis.'
non fumum ex fulgore, sed ex fumo dare lucem
cogitat, ut speciosa dehinc miracula promat,
Antiphaten, Scyllamque et cum Cyclope Charybdin.

Obey the conventions, or if you make something new,
Be sure it stays true to itself. If in your play
You're bringing back the embassy to Achilles,
Make him bitter, and stubborn, impetuous, irascible;
If it's Medea, ferocious and implacable;
Let Ino weep, Ixion be treacherous,
Io a wanderer, Orestes mournful.
But if you want to venture on your own
And introduce a new character to the stage,
Be sure he's recognizably the same
Person he was at the end as at the beginning;
Be sure, that is, he's always self-consistent.
It's hard to pretend to be the first to sing
About the things we all experience;
It's better to make your poem from matter of Troy
Than try for utter originality,
For if you don't just lazily saunter about
On the easy paths of the public domain you'll earn
Your rightful ownership of part of it,
So long as you're not a pedissequous slave
Following foot for foot one foot at a time
Into the trap of timorous hyper-correctness.

And don't begin your poem the way the old
Cyclic "Homeric" poets saw fit to do it:
"I sing of the famous war and Priam's fate."
What's to come out of the mouth of such a boaster?
The mountain labored and brought forth a mouse.
Ridiculous. He does much better who doesn't
Try so hard or make such grandiose claims:
"Muse, tell me about the man who, after Troy,
Witnessed the ways of men in other places."
His aim is light from smoke, not smoke from fire,
To make the wonders he tells of—Scylla, Charybdis,
Antiphates, the Cyclops—shine more brightly.
To tell Diomedes' story he doesn't think
He has to start with the death of the hero's uncle,
Or start, in telling about the Trojan War,

Nec reditum Diomedis ab interitu Meleagri
nec gemino bellum Troianum orditur ab ovo.
semper ad eventum festinat et in medias res
non secus ac notas auditorem rapit, et quae
desperat tractata nitescere posse relinquit,
atque ita mentitur, sic veris falsa remiscet,
primo ne medium, medio ne discrepet imum.

Tu quid ego et populus mecum desideret audi:
si plausoris eges aulaea manentis et usque
sessuri donec cantor 'vos plaudite' dicat,
aetatis cuiusque notandi sunt tibi mores
mobilibusque decor naturis dandus et annis.
reddere qui voces iam scit puer et pede certo
signat humum, gestit paribus colludere, et iram
concipit ac ponit temere et mutatur in horas.
imberbis iuvenis, tandem custode remoto,
gaudet equis canibusque et aprici gramine Campi,
cereus in vitium flecti, monitoribus asper,
utilium tardus provisor, prodigus aeris,
sublimis cupidusque et amata relinquere pernix.
conversis studiis aetas animusque virilis
quaerit opes et amicitias, inservit honori,
commisisse cavet quod mox mutare laboret.
multa senem circumveniunt incommoda, vel quod
quaerit et inventis miser abstinet ac timet uti
vel quod res omnis timide gelideque ministrat,
dilator, spe longus, iners avidusque futuri,

By telling us how Helen came out of an egg.
He goes right to the point and carries the reader
Into the midst of things, as if known already;
And if there's material that he despairs of presenting
So as to shine for us, he leaves it out;
And he makes his whole poem one. What's true, what's invented,
Beginning, middle, and end, all fit together.

Here's what the public expects, and so do I:
If you want to be sure of our approval, so that
We'll wait for the curtain and stay in our seats until
It's time for the singer to say it's time to applaud,
You have to be a careful observer of how
People really behave at their different ages,
And suit your treatment to what you have observed.
The little kid who's recently learned to talk
And learned to walk and not just unsteadily toddle,
Loves to play games with his little mates, and has
Plenty of fits and tantrums, and, just like that,
Quick as a wink, they're over. The beardless youth,
Glad to be rid of his tutor, loves to be out
On the grass of the sunny Campus, loves horses and hounds;
He's as yielding as softest wax to the imprint of vice,
But testy and stubborn when somebody offers wise counsel,
Imprudent about the future, careless with money,
Passionate—and confused—in his desires.
Contrary to this, the grown man knows exactly
The rewards he seeks, in influence, and money,
And single-mindedly works on how to get them,
Though he's wary of being involved in anything
That he thinks might possibly later have to be changed.
An old man has lots of problems: for instance, he's
Accumulated money and now he gets
No pleasure from it at all, he's so afraid
To let any of it go, and he's like that
In everything he does, cold, timid, slow,
Fearful of the future, afraid to die,
Difficult, querulous, disparaging the young
While full of praise for the days of his own lost youth.

difficilis, querulus, laudator temporis acti
se puero, castigator censorque minorum.
multa ferunt anni venientes commoda secum,
multa recedentes adimunt. ne forte seniles
mandentur iuveni partes pueroque viriles,
semper in adiunctis aevoque morabimur aptis.

Aut igitur res in scaenis aut acta refertur.
segnius irritant animos demissa per aurem
quam quae sunt oculis subiecta fidelibus et quae
ipse sibi tradit spectator. non tamen intus
digna geri promes in scaenam, multaque tolles
ex oculis quae mox narret facundia praesens.
ne pueros coram populo Medea trucidet
aut humana palam coquat extra nefarius Atreus
aut in avem Procne vertatur, Cadmus in anguem.
quodcumque ostendis mihi sic, incredulus odi.

Neve minor neu sit quinto productior actu
fabula, quae posci vult et spectanda reposci.
nec deus intersit, nisi dignus vindice nodus
inciderit; nec quartá loqui persona laboret.
actoris partis chorus officiumque virile
defendat; neu quid medios intercinat actus
quod non proposito conducat et haereat apte.
ille bonis faveatque et consilietur amice
et regat iratos et amet peccare timentis;
ille dapes laudet mensae brevis, ille salubrem
iustitiam legesque et apertis otia portis;
ille tegat commissa deosque precetur et oret
ut redeat miseris, abeat Fortuna superbis.

So let's not mix things up, giving an old
Gentleman a young man's attributes,
Or making a child seem like he's middle-aged.
Let's keep to a sense of what's appropriate.

An event gets acted out or it gets narrated.
Generally speaking the mind is more excited
By what it actually sees with its own eyes
Than by what comes in through the avenues of the ears.
Yet there are things it's better not to see
Enacted on the stage in front of you;
Better to have an actor tell you about them.
Medea ought not to slaughter her babies onstage
Nor Atreus cook his dish of human flesh,
Nor Procne be transformed into a bird
Nor Cadmus into a serpent. Things like this
Are incredible or revolting if shown directly.

Let your play be five acts long, no more, no less,
If you ever want it staged a second time.
And unless the crisis is really up to it
Don't call upon a god to come in and solve it.
Three actors speaking on stage are quite enough
At any one moment. And the chorus should be an actor,
Sustaining its part in the play as the others do;
Nothing the chorus sings between the acts
Should fail to carry forward the design;
Nothing it sings should be irrelevant;
As the friend of man it should counsel and side with the good,
Seek to restrain the violent from his deed,
Support the person who's fearful of doing wrong.
The chorus should praise the life of moderation,
Praise justice, and order, and peace that opens the gates;
The chorus, bystander, should keep the secrets it knows,
And pray to the gods that fortune depart from the haughty,
Bestowing its favors once more on those who are wretched.

Time was when the flute put out no claim to vie,
As it does today, with the brassy noisy trumpet;

Tibia non, ut nunc, orichalco vincta tubaeque
aemula, sed tenuis simplexque foramine pauco
aspirare et adesse choris erat utilis atque
nondum spissa nimis complere sedilia flatu;
quo sane populus numerabilis, utpote parvus,
et frugi castusque verecundusque coibat.
postquam coepit agros extendere victor et urbem
latior amplecti murus vinoque diurno
placari Genius festis impune diebus,
accessit numerisque modisque licentia maior.
indoctus quid enim saperet liberque laborum
rusticus urbano confusus, turpis honesto?
sic priscae motumque et luxuriam addidit arti
tibicen traxitque vagus per pulpita vestem;
sic etiam fidibus voces crevere severis
et tulit eloquium insolitum facundia praeceps
utiliumque sagax rerum et divina futuri
sortilegis non discrepuit sententia Delphis.

Carmine qui tragico vilem certavit ob hircum,
mox etiam agrestis Satyros nudavit et asper
incolumi gravitate iocum temptavit, eo quod
illecebris erat et grata novitate morandus
spectator, functusque sacris et potus et exlex.
verum ita risores, ita commendare dicaces
conveniet Satyros, ita vertere seria ludo,
ne quicumque deus, quicumque adhibebitur heros,
regali conspectus in auro nuper et ostro,
migret in obscuras humili sermone tabernas,
aut, dum vitat humum, nubes et inania captet.

The flute was slender then, and simply made,
With just a few stops, perfectly fit for the task
Of leading the chorus and making its music heard
Across the few rows of benches which were then
All that there were, and not very crowded either—
Easy to tell how few, because so few.
And the audience was modest, rational, decent.
But then when cities expanded and took in more
Of the countryside, and when there was no fine,
On festival days, for drinking in the daytime,
The times and its music changed a lot, for the worse.
What would you expect, when ignorant rustics,
Just come in from the farm, crowd into the stalls
And jostle and elbow their town-bred betters there.
The flute-player added to his pristine arts
New gestures and new flourishes and such,
And sashayed around the stage, trailing his gown;
Just so was the austere music of the lyre
Now swollen and elaborated too;
And a new undisciplined rhetoric came in
And brought in with it strange new ways of speaking,
Riddlingly prophetic of the future,
Full of inscrutable Delphic oracular wisdom.
The poet who used to try to win the goat prize
With simple tragic matter soon got away with
Bringing naked satyrs right into his scenes,
Serious and unserious jumbled together,
For novelty alone could charm and please
A holiday drunken lawless audience.
But the right way to do it, if really what you want
Is to bring in satyrs, is to do it so that, when
You move from grave to funny, no god or hero
Who's just been seen in dignified gold and purple
Will all of a sudden be found in a low-life tavern
Speaking a low-life language, nor will he be seen—
Ludicrous—up in the air, snatching at clouds.
Tragedy shouldn't be asked to prattle away
In trifling verses; she'd be like a shamefaced matron

effutire levis indigna tragoedia versus,
ut festis matrona moveri iussa diebus,
intererit Satyris paulum pudibunda protervis.
non ego inornata et dominantia nomina solum
verbaque, Pisones, Satyrorum scriptor amabo;
nec sic enitar tragico differre colori
ut nihil intersit Davusne loquatur et audax
Pythias emuncto lucrata Simone talentum,
an custos famulusque dei Silenus alumni.
ex noto fictum carmen sequar, ut sibi quivis
speret idem, sudet multum frustraque laboret
ausus idem: tantum series iuncturaque pollet,
tantum de medio sumptis accedit honoris.
silvis deducti caveant, me iudice, Fauni
ne velut innati triviis ac paene forenses
aut nimium teneris iuvenentur versibus umquam
aut immunda crepent ignominiosaque dicta.
offenduntur enim quibus est equus et pater et res,
nec, si quid fricti ciceris probat et nucis emptor,
aequis accipiunt animis donantque corona.

Syllaba longa brevi subiecta vocatur iambus,
pes citus; unde etiam trimetris accrescere iussum
nomen iambeis, cum senos redderet ictus
primus ad extremum similis sibi. non ita pridem
tardior ut paulo graviorque veniret ad auris,
spondeos stabilis in iura paterna recepit
commodus et patiens, non ut de sede secunda
cederet aut quarta socialiter. hic et in Acci
nobilibus trimetris apparet rarus et Enni

Forced to get up and join some holiday dance
Along with the shameless dancing naked satyrs.

If I decided to write a satyr-play,
Pisos, you wouldn't find me confining myself
To a low colloquial style; when it was right,
You wouldn't find me avoiding a higher tone,
As if it didn't make any difference whether
Davus was talking to Pythias, who's just conned
Simo out of his money, or whether he's talking
To Dionysus's guardian servant, Silenus.
My aim is to take familiar things and make
Poetry of them, and do it in such a way
That it looks as if it was easy as could be
For anybody to do it (although he'd sweat
And strain and work his head off, all in vain).
Such is the power of judgment, of knowing what
It means to put the elements together
In just the right way; such is the power of making
A perfectly wonderful thing out of nothing much.
When the fauns come in from the forest to be onstage
They shouldn't be made to act as if they were born
And grew up in the marketplace, singing gross songs
And telling each other obscene disgusting jokes.
Some people there won't like it, the gentlemen,
The heads of households, the solid citizens,
Who can't be expected to greet with approbation
The things the popcorn buyers seem to fall for.

A short and then a long is called an iambus,
Light on its feet; iambic trimeter
Is called by that name though it's really made of six
Unvaried steady beats that move along the line;
But spondees were recently admitted so
The line might move more slowly and more gravely
(How slow, the spondees moving along, how slow,
Though not allowed in the second foot or fourth).
Old Accius in his well-known trimeters seldom
Used the iambic foot, nor Ennius either,

in scaenam missos cum magno pondere versus
aut operae celeris nimium curaque carentis
aut ignoratae premit artis crimine turpi.

Non quivis videt immodulata poemata iudex
et data Romanis venia est indigna poetis.
idcircone vager scribamque licenter? an omnis
visuros peccata putem mea, tutus et intra
spem veniae cautus? vitavi denique culpam:
non laudem merui. vos exemplaria Graeca
nocturna versate manu, versate diurna.
at vestri proavi Plautinos et numeros et
laudavere sales, nimium patienter utrumque,
ne dicam stulte, mirati, si modo ego et vos
scimus inurbanum lepido seponere dicto
legitimumque sonum digitis callemus et aure.

Ignotum tragicae genus invenisse Camenae
dicitur et plaustris vexisse poemata Thespis
qui canerent agerentque peruncti faucibus ora.
post hunc personae pallaeque repertor honestae
Aeschylus et modicis instravit pulpita tignis
et docuit magnumque loqui nitique cothurno.
successit vetus his comoedia, non sine multa
laude; sed in vitium libertas excidit et vim
dignam lege regi. lex est accepta chorusque
turpiter obticuit sublato iure nocendi.

Battering the boards with pounding of ponderous verses
Produced either with hasty carelessness
Or because he knew too little about his craft.
Not everybody knows enough to tell
When verses are unmusical, and so
Our Roman poets have found it very easy
To think they've been given permission to be slack.
Does that mean *I* am free to be licentious?
Or does it mean I should assume that all
The faults I have will be apparent to all
And therefore I should warily write so as
To have some hope of getting through unblamed.
(The most I can say is not that I've been praised,
But that I've gotten through more or less unblamed.)
So, study Grecian models night and day.
Your ancestors, you tell me, lavished praise
On Plautus, both for his wit and his versification.
But if we learn how to tell coarse speech apart
From elegant speech, and also if we learn
By ear and by finger-count to discern true music,
We'd have to say their praise was foolish and lax.

The theretofore nonexistent Tragic genre
Was first invented, so they say, by Thespis,
Whose players went from town to town on wagons,
Their faces painted with the lees of wine.
Then Aeschylus came along and built a little
Platform for his buskined players wearing
The masks and beautiful costumes he'd devised;
He taught them high deportment and lofty speech.
Old Comedy came next, worthy of praise,
But its liberty turned into license, its force
Into violence and riot, and the law
Rightly was invoked and was obeyed,
And the Chorus, shamed, was silenced, rendered harmless.

Our Roman poets have tried every style there is,
Nor have they least deserved the praise they've won
When they have had the audacity to stray

Nil intemptatum nostri liquere poetae,
nec minimum meruere decus vestigia Graeca
ausi deserere et celebrare domestica facta
vel qui praetextas vel qui docuere togatas.
nec virtute foret clarisque potentius armis
quam lingua Latium, si non offenderet unum
quemque poetarum limae labor et mora. vos, o
Pompilius sanguis, carmen reprehendite quod non
multa dies et multa litura coercuit atque
perfectum decies non castigavit ad unguem.
ingenium misera quia fortunatius arte
credit et excludit sanos Helicone poetas
Democritus, bona pars non unguis ponere curat,
non barbam, secreta petit loca, balnea vitat.
nanciscetur enim pretium nomenque poeta
si tribus Anticyris caput insanabile numquam
tonsori Licino commiserit. o ego laevus,
qui purgor bilem sub verni temporis horam!
non alius faceret meliora poemata. verum
nil tanti est. ergo fungar vice cotis, acutum
reddere quae ferrum valet exsors ipsa secandi;
munus et officium nil scribens ipse docebo,
unde parentur opes, quid alat formetque poetam,
quid deceat, quid non, quo virtus, quo ferat error.

Scribendi recte sapere est et principium et fons.
rem tibi Socraticae poterunt ostendere chartae
verbaque provisam rem non invita sequentur.

From Grecian paths in order to celebrate
The deeds of Rome upon the Roman stage.
Nor would Rome be more glorious for its deeds
Of valor and of conquest than for its letters
If it weren't that every last one of our poets lacked
The patience to put up with the tedious business
Of using the polishing file. Descendants of Numa,
Withhold your favor from any poem that doesn't
Show signs of the time spent upon it, the blotting, and pruning,
The cutting, amending, putting the polished surface
Ten times over again to the fingernail's test.
Democritus taught that inborn genius is
Worth much much more than poor old hard-earned skill,
And he shut the door to Helicon to any
Poet who happened to be in his right mind,
And, ever since, there are lots of poets who wouldn't
Dream of cutting their nails or shaving their beards,
And love to hang around in lonely haunts
Far from the public baths. The way to gain
A poetic reputation is, never entrust
To any barbershop the shaggy head
That hellebore, the madness medicine, couldn't
In dosage after dosage possibly cure.

What a fool I am for purging myself of bile
Each year as soon as Spring comes round again.
Nobody would write better poems than I
If I didn't do so. But what on earth's the point?
Instead I'll choose to be a kind of whetstone,
Good for sharpening steel to a cutting edge,
But itself unable to cut. Though I write nothing
I'll teach what it is to write, what fosters a poet
And makes him what he is; what's right; what's wrong;
What paths he ought or ought not to set out on.
The source and resource of writing well is knowledge.
Wise books are full of knowledge and once you've learned
From reading them, then surely words will follow.
The man who's learned what's owing to his country
And to his friends, and the love he ought to feel

qui didicit patriae quid debeat et quid amicis,
quo sit amore parens, quo frater amandus et hospes,
quod sit conscripti, quod iudicis officium, quae
partes in bellum missi ducis, ille profecto
reddere personae scit convenientia cuique.
respicere exemplar vitae morumque iubebo
doctum imitatorem et vivas hinc ducere voces.
interdum speciosa locis morataque recte
fabula nullius Veneris sed pondere inerti
valdius oblectat populum meliusque moratur
quam versus inopes rerum nugaeque canorae.

Grais ingenium, Grais dedit ore rotundo
Musa loqui, praeter laudem nullius avaris.
Romani pueri longis rationibus assem
discunt in partis centum diducere. 'dicat
filius Albani: si de quincunce remota est
uncia, quid superat? poteras dixisse.' 'triens.' 'eu!
rem poteris servare tuam. redit uncia: quid fit?'
'semis.' an, haec animos aerugo et cura peculi
cum semel imbuerit, speremus carmina fingi
posse linenda cedro et levi servanda cupresso?

Aut prodesse volunt aut delectare poetae
aut simul et iucunda et idonea dicere vitae.
quidquid praecipies, esto brevis, ut cito dicta
percipiant animi dociles teneantque fideles.
omne supervacuum pleno de pectore manat.
ficta voluptatis causa sint proxima veris:
ne quodcumque velit poscat sibi fabula credi,
neu pransae Lamiae vivum puerum extrahat alvo.

For a parent, a brother, or for a welcome guest,
And knows what the obligations of a judge
Or of a statesman are, and knows the way
A general who's in battle ought to behave,
Will have the means to portray them properly.
My advice to the writer who thus is well-prepared
Is that he carefully observe what life
And manners seen firsthand are really like
And bring their voices back alive in words.
It's even true that a rather humdrum play,
So long as there's truth of observation shown,
If only in certain passages, can often
Hold the attention better and give more pleasure
Than pretty-sounding verses empty of meaning.

The Muse gave genius to the Greeks, and the power to speak
With eloquent voices; glory was all they sought for.
We Romans spend our childhoods doing our sums.
"Tell me, Albanus's son, from five-twelfths take
One-twelfth away, how much is left? Speak up."
"One-third, sir." "Good! I see you're going to be
A competent manager of your property.
Now add a twelfth to five-twelfths, what do you get?"
"A half." Tell me, when once this pettiness
Corrupts the soul, how *could* there be any hope
For poetry to be written worth preserving
With cedar oil in polished cypress boards?

Poetry wants to instruct or else to delight;
Or, better still, to delight and instruct at once.
As for instruction, make it succinct, so the mind
Can quickly seize on what's being taught and hold it;
Every superfluous word spills out of a full mind.
As for delight, in what you invent stay close
To actuality; your fable shouldn't
Feel free to ask your audience to credit
Just anything whatsoever, no matter what:
Produce no human babies from monsters' bellies.
The elders in the audience reject

centuriae seniorum agitant expertia frugis,
celsi praetereunt austera poemata Ramnes.
omne tulit punctum qui miscuit utile dulci,
lectorem delectando pariterque monendo.
hic meret aera liber Sosiis; hic et mare transit
et longum noto scriptori prorogat aevum.

Sunt delicta tamen quibus ignovisse velimus;
nam neque chorda sonum reddit quem vult manus et mens
poscentique gravem persaepe remittit acutum
nec semper feriet quodcumque minabitur arcus.
verum ubi plura nitent in carmine, non ego paucis
offendar maculis, quas aut incuria fudit
aut humana parum cavit natura. quid ergo est?
ut scriptor si peccat idem librarius usque,
quamvis est monitus, venia caret; ut citharoedus
ridetur chorda qui semper oberrat eadem:
sic mihi qui multum cessat fit Choerilus ille,
quem bis terve bonum cum risu miror; et idem
indignor quandoque bonus dormitat Homerus;
verum operi longo fas est obrepere somnum.

Ut pictura poesis: erit quae, si propius stes,
te capiat magis, et quaedam, si longius abstes.
haec amat obscurum, volet haec sub luce videri,
iudicis argutum quae non formidat acumen;
haec placuit semel, haec decies repetita placebit.

O maior iuvenum, quamvis et voce paterna
fingeris ad rectum et per te sapis, hoc tibi dictum
tolle memor, certis medium et tolerabile rebus

The work that yields no profitable wisdom,
The young aristocrats what yields no pleasure.
He who provides to all both profit and pleasure
Wins everybody's vote: his book will bring
Money for bookstore owners and fame across
The seas and down the years to the author himself.

Certainly there are faults we'd overlook:
Sometimes the lyre string doesn't produce the sound
The mind and hand intended, and so the grave
Deep dignified tone you tried for suddenly screeches;
Sometimes the arrow aimed at the bull's-eye misses.
When most things shine in a song, then I'm not bothered
At all if there are blemishes here or there
That carelessness or frailty have let happen.
But here's what I mean to say: you'd blame a scribe
Who time and time again made the same error,
No matter how many times he'd been told about it;
You'd ridicule the harpist who botched the same passage
Over and over; just as with them, the poet
Who blunders like Choerilus most of the time
Is the object of wonder and laughter whenever, by chance,
He writes a good line. It's true that it bothers me
When Homer nods, but, after all, it's true
That writers of such long works *must* drowse sometimes.

With poems it's as with pictures; one pleases you more
The closer you stand; another pleases you more
The farther from it you are. The first one loves
To be seen in shadow; the other to be in the light
And has no fear of the judge's close critique.
The first gave pleasure once and only once;
The other, ten times seen, will still give pleasure.
O eldest brother, brought up by your father
To judge things rightly (and being wise yourself),
Learn this dictum by heart and heed it well:
Not everything can get away with being
No more than tolerable, no more than so-so.

recte concedi. consultus iuris et actor
causarum mediocris abest virtute diserti
Messallae nec scit quantum Cascellius Aulus,
sed tamen in pretio est: mediocribus esse poetis
non homines, non di, non concessere columnae.
ut gratas inter mensas symphonia discors
et crassum unguentum et Sardo cum melle papaver
offendunt, poterat duci quia cena sine istis,
sic animis natum inventumque poema iuvandis,
si paulum summo decessit, vergit ad imum.
ludere qui nescit, campestribus abstinet armis
indoctusque pilae discive trochive quiescit,
ne spissae risum tollant impune coronae:
qui nescit versus tamen audet fingere. quidni?
liber et ingenuus, praesertim census equestrem
summam nummorum vitioque remotus ab omni.
tu nihil invita dices faciesve Minerva;
id tibi iudicium est, ea mens. si quid tamen olim
scripseris, in Maeci descendat iudicis auris
et patris et nostras nonumque prematur in annum
membranis intus positis. delere licebit
quod non edideris; nescit vox missa reverti.

Silvestris homines sacer interpresque deorum
caedibus et victu foedo deterruit Orpheus,
dictus ob hoc lenire tigris rabidosque leones;

A lawyer who's just o.k. can, maybe, lack
The eloquence of Messalla or the learning
Of Cascellius, and, nevertheless, perform
Some useful functions. However, a poet who's
Just mediocre, just all right, has nothing
Of any value to bring to men or gods.
It's as when at a party the music's played
Discordantly, the perfumed oil is viscous,
The poppy seeds are served with second-rate honey:
The offense is that the feast could get along
Without ineptitudes like these. A poem's
Created to yield delight to the heart and mind.
If it falls a little short of doing that,
It falls right down to the bottom, all the way down.
The youth who doesn't know how to play the martial
Games they play on the Campus Martius wouldn't
Be caught dead putting on armor and trying; and he
Who isn't good with discus, ball, or hoop
Stays out of the game, for fear of being laughed at.
But he who hasn't a clue about writing a poem
Feels perfectly at liberty to write one.
Why not? He's free, free-*born*, maybe even
A knight in good repute, and with plenty of money.
Certainly *you* have too much sense and judgment
To do anything that might offend Minerva.
But if you ever venture to write a poem,
Submit it to the critical ears of Tarpa,
Or to your father's, or to mine; and then
Put it away someplace for, say, nine years.
You can always tear up what you haven't published yet;
Once published you could never take it back.

In the days when men still wandered in the woods,
Orpheus, holy interpreter of the gods,
Taught us to shun the life of blood and killing.
Therefore there's the story of how his music
Tamed the ravening beasts, the lions and tigers;
And there's the story too of how the trance

dictus et Amphion, Thebanae conditor urbis,
saxa movere sono testudinis et prece blanda
ducere quo vellet. fuit haec sapientia quondam,
publica privatis secernere, sacra profanis,
concubitu prohibere vago, dare iura maritis,
oppida moliri, leges incidere ligno.
sic honor et nomen divinis vatibus atque
carminibus venit. post hos insignis Homerus
Tyrtaeusque mares animos in Martia bella
versibus exacuit; dictae per carmina sortes
et vitae monstrata via est et gratia regum
Pieriis temptata modis ludusque repertus
et longorum operum finis, ne forte pudori
sit tibi Musa lyrae sollers et cantor Apollo.

Natura fieret laudabile carmen an arte
quaesitum est. ego nec studium sine divite vena
nec rude quid prosit video ingenium; alterius sic
altera poscit opem res et coniurat amice.
qui studet optatam cursu contingere metam
multa tulit fecitque puer, sudavit et alsit,
abstinuit Venere et vino; qui Pythia certat
tibicen, didicit prius extimuitque magistrum.
an satis est dixisse 'ego mira poemata pango.
occupet extremum scabies; mihi turpe relinqui est
et quod non didici sane nescire fateri?'

Of Amphion playing his enchanting music
Caused the stones to move and rise and go
To do his bidding, building the walls of Thebes.
This was the wisdom of song in days gone by:
To know how to tell the difference between
Public and private, the sacred and the profane;
To curb licentiousness and put in place
The rules of marriage; establish cities and
On wooden tablets write down settled laws.
Thus honor and glory as to divinities came
To the earliest poets and to the songs they sang.
Then it was famous Homer's time, and time
For Tyrtaeus to rouse men up with his martial verse
To glorious battle; oracles spoke in song;
The way to live was taught to men in music;
Music tempered the haughtiness of kings;
And offered delight at the end of the long day's toil.
We need not be ashamed of how the Muse
Accompanies on her lyre Apollo singing.

The question often comes up, whether a good
Poem derives from nature or from art?
The truth of it is, learning is nothing at all
Without the bounty of nature, and natural talent
Is nothing at all if left to itself untaught.
Each has to depend on the other, and so together
They do the work as friends. The runner who wants
To win the race has, since he was a boy,
Put up with a lot in training, has sweated and strained,
And kept himself away from wine and women.
The flutist who wants to play at the Pythian games
Studies his lessons hard, scared of his teacher.
But poets today find it perfectly easy to say,
"I love this poem I wrote; it's wonderful!
I'm the king of the hill." They wouldn't dream
Of being left behind or of confessing
That they hadn't learned what they hadn't tried to learn.

Ut praeco, ad merces turbam qui cogit emendas,
assentatores iubet ad lucrum ire poeta
dives agris, dives positis in faenore nummis.
si vero est unctum qui recte ponere possit
et spondere levi pro paupere et eripere artis
litibus implicitum, mirabor si sciet inter-
noscere mendacem verumque beatus amicum.
tu seu donaris seu quid donare voles cui,
nolito ad versus tibi factos ducere plenum
laetitiae: clamabit enim 'pulchre! bene! recte!'
pallescet super his, etiam stillabit amicis
ex oculis rorem, saliet, tundet pede terram.
ut qui conducti plorant in funere dicunt
et faciunt prope plura dolentibus ex animo, sic
derisor vero plus laudatore movetur.
reges dicuntur multis urgere culillis
et torquere mero quem perspexisse laborent,
an sit amicitia dignus: si carmina condes,
numquam te fallant animi sub vulpe latentes.

Quintilio si quid recitares, 'corrige, sodes,
hoc' aiebat 'et hoc.' melius te posse negares,
bis terque expertum frustra delere iubebat
et male tornatos incudi reddere versus.
si defendere delictum quam vertere malles,
nullum ultra verbum aut operam insumebat inanem,
quin sine rivali teque et tua solus amares.
vir bonus et prudens versus reprehendet inertis,
culpabit duros, incomptis allinet atrum
traverso calamo signum, ambitiosa recidet
ornamenta, parum claris lucem dare coget,
arguet ambigue dictum, mutanda notabit,

Just as an auctioneer calls out to gather
A crowd to show off his goods to, so a rich poet
Calls on his flatterers all to gather round him.
But if there's something in it for them, a good dinner,
Security for a loan, or help with a lawsuit,
How will he ever tell who's true and who's false?
If by any chance you've given someone a present
Or let him know of your intent to give one,
Don't ask that delighted person in to hear
The verses you've just written. He's sure to cry out,
"Beautiful! Oh marvelous! Just perfect!,"
Keep time to your meters with his excited feet,
Turn pale with sympathetic feeling, weep.
A hired mourner at a funeral's likely
To sob and gesticulate more than the truly bereaved;
So he who's secretly derisive shows
More feeling than a true admirer would.
It's said that a king who wants to see into a man,
To see who he is, test if he's worthy of trust,
Will offer him cup after cup of wine, to find out.
If you want to write poems, don't let yourself be fooled
By what the fox foxily hides from you.

If Quintilius read a manuscript of yours,
He'd say, "Please, if you will, change this, and this,"
And if, after you tried and failed to make
The corrections he'd advised you to make, he'd tell you
To tear it up and take it back to the forge
To be remade. And if you got defensive
And wouldn't even try, he wouldn't say
Another word or waste another minute,
To come between yourself and your self-love.
A forthright reasonable man will tell you
Candidly when you've written lifeless verses,
Or harsh or graceless verses; he'll take his pen
And draw a firm black line right straight across them;
He'll excise fancy writing; he'll demand
That you clarify what's ambiguous or obscure;

fiet Aristarchus; nec dicet 'cur ego amicum
offendam in nugis?' hae nugae seria ducent
in mala derisum semel exceptumque sinistre.

Ut mala quem scabies aut morbus regius urget
aut fanaticus error et iracunda Diana,
vesanum tetigisse timent fugiuntque poetam
qui sapiunt: agitant pueri incautique sequuntur.
hic, dum sublimis versus ructatur et errat,
si veluti merulis intentus decidit auceps
in puteum foveamve, licet 'succurrite' longum
clamet, 'io cives!' non sit qui tollere curet.
si curet quis opem ferre et demittere funem,
'qui scis an prudens huc se proiecerit atque
servari nolit?' dicam, Siculique poetae
narrabo interitum. deus immortalis haberi
dum cupit Empedocles, ardentem frigidus Aetnam
insiluit. sit ius liceatque perire poetis.
invitum qui servat, idem facit occidenti.
non semel hoc fecit, nec, si retractus erit, iam
fiet homo et ponet famosae mortis amorem.
nec satis apparet cur versus factitet, utrum
minxerit in patrios cineres an triste bidental
moverit incestus; certe furit ac velut ursus,
obiectos caveae valuit si frangere clathros,
indoctum doctumque fugat recitator acerbus.
quem vero arripuit, tenet occiditque legendo,
non missura cutem nisi plena cruoris hirudo.

He'll make a mark wherever a change is needed;
He'll be an Aristarchus. He'll never say,
"Why should I hurt the feelings of a friend
Over such little things?" Such "little things"
Are serious matters if the work of his friend
Is going to be the object of derision.

Sensible people run from the crazy poet,
As afraid to touch him as if he had the itch,
Or the king's disease, or Diana's lunatic frenzy;
The little children follow him around
Jeering and taunting. He wanders around the landscape
Babbling verses, staring up at the sky,
And if, like a birder intent on sighting a bird,
He happens to fall down into a well or a pit,
He calls out "Citizens, help!" and nobody comes,
Or else if somebody comes to pull him out,
"What if he doesn't want to be helped?," I say.
"What if he fell in the well of his own free will?
What if he did it on purpose?" And then I tell them
About the Sicilian poet, Empedocles,
Who cool as can be hopped into the hot volcano.
Such poets have the right to do themselves in;
To save one may be to him like killing him off.
This poet isn't the first one to fall down a well,
And if you pull him out there's no guarantee
He's therefore going to be a sensible person
And give up his wish to die a famous death.

What made him become a poet, anyway?
Maybe he pissed on the ashes of his father
Or did something else unholy someplace holy.
Whatever it was, he's crazy, and, like a bear
Who's broken out of his cage, he puts to flight
Everybody he meets by his horrible reading.
If he catches a man, he'll read that man to *death*.
He's a leech that won't let go till he's full of blood.

ACKNOWLEDGMENTS

NOTES

GLOSSARY

ACKNOWLEDGMENTS

Some of the epistles have previously appeared in *The American Poetry Review, Arion, Literary Imagination, Partisan Review, Persephone, Slate, Tin House, TriQuarterly* (a publication of Northwestern University), and *Of No Country I Know: New and Selected Poems* (David Ferry; University of Chicago Press, 1999).

I have of course consulted a number of other translations and a number of commentaries. I am especially indebted for help to: H. Rushton Fairclough, ed. and trans., *Horace: Satires, Epistles and Ars Poetica*, The Loeb Classical Library (Cambridge, Mass.: Harvard University Press, 1966); C. O. Brink, *Horace on Poetry*, 3 vols. (Cambridge, Eng.: Cambridge University Press, 1963–82); Smith Palmer Bovie, trans., *Satires and Epistles of Horace* (Chicago: Chicago University Press, 1959); Jacob Fuchs, trans., *Horace's Satires and Epistles* (New York: W. W. Norton, 1977); Kenneth J. Reckford, *Horace* (New York: Twayne, 1969); Niall Rudd, ed., *Horace: Epistles Book II and Epistle to the Pisones (Ars Poetica)* (Cambridge, Eng.: Cambridge University Press, 1989); Roland Myer, ed., *Horace: Epistles, Vol. I* (Cambridge, Eng.: Cambridge University Press, 1994); W. R. Johnson, *Horace and the Dialectic of Freedom: Readings in Epistles I* (Ithaca, N.Y.: Cornell University Press, 1993); Ellen Oliensis, *Horace and the Rhetoric of Authority* (Cambridge, Eng.: Cambridge University Press, 1998); David Armstrong, *Horace* (New Haven: Yale University Press, 1989); Reuben A. Brower, *Alexander Pope: The Poetry of Allusion* (Oxford: Clarendon Press, 1959). For help with the Glossary I am indebted to J. E. Zimmerman, *Dictionary of Classical Mythology* (New York: Harper and Row, 1964).

The list of friends—poets and critics—who have helped me is too long to list here. I owe special thanks to those who have answered my many questions about Horace's Latin: Donald Carne-Ross, Wendell Clausen, John Cobb, Rodney Dennis, Kenneth Haynes, Patricia Johnson, Miranda Marvin, Larry Rosenwald, Stephen Scully, Raymond Starr, Rosanna Warren.

I'm deeply grateful to the editorial staff at Farrar, Straus and Giroux, especially Jonathan Galassi and Karla Reganold, and the designers, Abby Kagan and Cynthia Krupat; and also Lorin Stein, James Wilson, Chandra Wohleber, Anne Coyle, and Andrea Joyce.

As always, I owe most to Anne Ferry.

NOTES

i.1   The first satire in Horace's earliest work, the first book of Satires, was addressed to his great patron and friend, Maecenas. His last poem, probably, was Epistle ii.1, addressed to the Emperor, Augustus.

"Down by the Arch of Janus": Down in the business district, in the Roman Forum.

"the bed . . . set up in the hall / Of the married man's house": The custom was to set the bed there to invoke the blessing and favor of the household Genius or personal god.

i.2   Nothing is known of Lollius Maximus except what can be inferred from this poem: that he was young, still studying in Rome; and from Epistle i.18, that he was an athlete, had served in the army in Spain, and was well-to-do. Maybe he belonged to the family of Marcus Lollius, consul, who is admiringly addressed in Horace's Ode iv.9.

i.3   Julius Florus is also addressed in the great second Epistle of Book Two. Nothing is known of him, or of Titius or Celsus, except what can be inferred from these two poems: that they were young, promising, literary in their interests, and on the staff of Tiberius, Augustus's stepson, who would become the second Emperor. In 20 B.C.E. Tiberius undertook a successful expedition that resulted in the conquering of Armenia.

Epistle i.8 is addressed to Celsus.

Apollo's library: Augustus established a library in the Temple of Apollo on the Palatine Hill above the Forum.

Nothing outside this poem is known about Munatius.

i.4   Cassius: The identity isn't certain. Perhaps a poet named Cassius Etruscus, whose work is criticized in Horace's Satire i.10.

i.5   Torquatus, evidently a lawyer, is probably the same friend addressed in Ode iv.7. It is said that Torquatus defended Moschus of Pergamum, a teacher of rhetoric, against accusations that he was a poisoner.

       The guests Butra, Septicus, and Sabinus are unknown outside the poem. Evidently there actually was an inexpensive furniture maker named Archias.

i.6   Nothing outside the poem is known about Numicius.

       "Tyrian cloths": Textiles from Tyre were highly prized.

       The Appian Way was a principal road out of Rome. Agrippa's colonnade was near the Pantheon, a place to be seen.

       "Influence": Suadela, the personification of persuasion.

       fasces: An ax tied into a bundle of sticks, signs of the office of a magistrate.

       In the second verse paragraph of my translation of this epistle, the lines beginning "Be early down at the Forum" (*navus mane Forum*) and ending "in admiration of him" (*mirabilis illi*) follow the order of the passage in H. Rushton Fairclough, ed., *Horace: Satires, Epistles and Ars Poetica*, The Loeb Classical Library (Cambridge, Mass.: Harvard University Press, 1966). In the Latin text used to accompany my translation, the lines can be found in the third verse paragraph.

i.7   Cynara: A conventional name. Cynara figures, later on, in Epistle i.14 and Odes iv.1 and iv.13.

       Philippus: L. Marcus Philippus was a famous lawyer and consul.

i.8   Celsus figures also in Epistle i.3.

       Nero: Tiberius, who was descended from the Nero family.

i.9   This Septimius may be the same friend addressed in Ode ii.6.

       Nero: See note to i.8.

i.10   Aristius Fuscus is the friend addressed in Ode i.22, *Integer vitae*.

       "live in accordance with / The nature of things": Stoic doctrine.

       The Dog Star is Canis, the Lion the constellation Leo.

       Dyes from the Phoenician city Sidon were highly admired; not so the domestic ones from Aquinum, a town near Rome.

i.11 Nothing is known about Bullatius outside this poem. Chios, Lesbos, Smyrna, Sardis, Colophon, Samos, Rhodes, Mitylene: Glamorous important foreign islands and cities in the Aegean and Asia Minor. Lebedus was also in Asia Minor, but not important. Gabii and Fidena were drab towns near Rome; Ulubrae also, which was notably marshy.

i.12 Iccius is the bookworm addressed in Ode i.29.

"*concordia discors*": Empedoclean doctrine, in which nature is a union of warring elements.

Pompeius Grosphus: The rich Sicilian landowner addressed in Ode ii.16.

Agrippa's valor: Agrippa's victory in Spain, Tiberius's annexing of Armenia, and the king of the Parthians, Phraates, returning in submission to Rome, all occurred at about the same time.

i.13 Vinius Asina: His last name means "donkey." He is said to have been an immensely big and strong (and therefore clumsy?) soldier.

The fiction or fact of the poem is that it was written when Horace was sending the first three volumes of the Odes to Augustus.

i.14 Lamia: A member of a prominent family. Perhaps this is Aelius Lamia, to whom Ode iii.15 is addressed.

Cynara: A conventional name. She figures also in Epistle i.7 and Odes iv.1 and iv.13.

i.15 Nothing is known about Numonius Vala outside the poem.

i.16 Quinctius: Probably Quinctius Hirpinus, a prominent friend of Horace's, addressed in Ode ii.11.

i.17 Scaeva: Nothing is known about him outside the poem. H. Rushton Fairclough, in the Loeb Library edition of the Epistles, points out that *scaevus* can mean "awkward."

"Not everyone has won his way to Corinth": A saying—"Not everyone is successful."

i.18 Lollius: See note to Epistle i.2.

"Miming line by line the words of the first": "In the mimes the actor playing second part commonly imitated the chief actor in word and gesture"—note in *Horace: Satires, Epistles, Ars Poetica*, ed. H. Rushton Fair-clough (Cambridge, Mass.: Loeb Classical Library, Harvard University, 1966), p. 369.

"The bond between / The Theban twins was nearly broken": This quarrel was between the sons of Zeus and Antiope. Together they built the city of Thebes. Zethus was a herdsman, Amphion a musician. Zethus carried the stones to the place and Amphion's music was a charm that ef-fortlessly caused the stones to rise up and become the walls.

"Actian battle": The brothers are replaying the sea battle between Antony and Octavian (Augustus) in 31 B.C.E.

i.19 "Libo's Well": A well in the Forum, where businessmen gathered. See Horace's Satire ii.6, where Horace is having fun scorning the grim sober business life of Rome. The particular reference is to line 35 of the Satire, but lines 59–76 are relevant.

"having no father-in-law": According to Horace, Archilochus wrote ragingly against Lycambes for obstructing Archilochus's attempts to marry Neobule, Lycambes's daughter. Neobule committed suicide.

"You're saving up your stuff / To read to Jove": That is, to the Em-peror, Augustus.

i.20 "Jason and Vertumnus": The place in the Forum where books were sold; and where prostitutes, male and female, gathered.

"far-off Africa . . . and . . . Spain": That is, to the Roman provinces.

Marcus Lollius and Aemilius Lepidus were consuls in 21 B.C.E.

ii.1 According to the biographer Gaius Tranquillus Suetonius (born about 69 A.D.), this epistle was written in response to the Emperor's complaint that Horace had written poems addressed to many other people but not to him.

Ennius's epic *Annales* opens with an account of a dream in which Homer tells Ennius that he, Ennius, is Homer reincarnate.

"Numa's Sicilian hymns": Incomprehensible hymns sung by an or-der of priests called the Salians. The hymns were traditionally supposed to have been composed by Numa Pompilius, second king of early Rome.

"And how would chaste boys and unwed maidens learn / The sup-pliant hymn they sing . . . ?": Horace is referring to his own *Carmen Sae-culare*, the poem he wrote at Augustus's command, to be sung at the Saecular Games in 17 B.C.E., by a choir of boys and girls.

"Tarentine": From Tarentum, in Apulia.

"Apollonian gift": The library Augustus established in the Temple of Apollo on the Palatine Hill.

"I'd much prefer to be able to be the teller / Of tales of heroic deeds . . .": In Odes 4, 14, 15, and others, Horace is in fact a teller of such tales, brilliantly, and it may be that he is referring directly to these poems. It also may be that Augustus had already read them. But Book Four of the Odes wasn't published till the year after the publication of Book Two of the Epistles, so we can't be sure.

ii.2   Julius Florus: Also addressed in Epistle i.3. See note.

"Philippi happened": Horace, when young, was involved in the battle at Philippi, 42 B.C.E., in which Brutus and the other assassins of Julius Caesar were defeated by Antony and Octavian (Augustus). Horace means here that his family lost property because of this and he had to write for a living. He did, however, procure a position in the Treasury and eventually, as a writer, became a member of the circle of those favored by Augustus.

ii.3   The Pisos: A prominent family, but nothing is known about this particular branch beyond what can be inferred from the poem. One of the two sons, at any rate, seems to have had ambitions to be a playwright.

The Aemilian School was a training school for gladiators.

"Raging Archilochus": See note to Epistle i.19.

Cyclic "Homeric" poets: Greek poets, much inferior to Homer, treating the Trojan War and related material. Only fragments survive.

"Muse, tell me about the man . . .": This echoes the opening lines of Homer's *Odyssey*.

"Scylla, Charybdis, / Antiphates, the Cyclops": These wonders are in Homer's *Odyssey*.

"the hero's uncle": Meleager was Diomedes' uncle.

"how Helen came out of an egg": Helen of Troy was the daughter of Zeus (as a swan) and Leda.

Davus, Pythias, Simo: Stock characters in comedy.

Silenus: Father of the satyrs; tutor of Dionysus.

"Old Comedy came next": Fifth century B.C.E. Greek comedy, such as the earlier plays of Aristophanes.

Pythian games: A musical and athletic competition held at Delphi in honor of Apollo.

GLOSSARY

ACCIUS: Lucius Accius, playwright, poet, and literary historian, born 170 B.C.E.

ACHILLES: The greatest of the warriors against Troy; slayer of Hector.

AESCHYLUS: Greek tragic poet, sixth century B.C.E.

AESOPUS: Tragic actor, first century B.C.E.

AFRANIUS: Lucius Afranius, second century B.C.E. comic playwright.

AGRIPPA: Marcus Vipsanius Agrippa was Augustus's chief military leader, by land and sea. He married Augustus's daughter Julia.

ALBAN MUSES: Local muses, the Alban Hills being the hills local to Rome.

ALCAEUS: Poet of the seventh century B.C.E., from the island of Lesbos. He fought against tyrants. Horace greatly admired his poems and adapted his meters to Latin.

ALCINOUS: Phaeacian king who sheltered Ulysses.

ANCUS: Ancus Martius, fourth king of Rome.

ANTENOR: An adviser to Priam, king of Troy.

ANTIPHATES: King of the Laestrygonians, the man-eating giants in Homer's *Odyssey*.

APELLES: Greek painter in the time of Alexander the Great, fourth century B.C.E.

APOLLO: Son of Zeus and Latona, brother of Diana. Born on the island of Delos. Sun god, god of the arts, god of healing, god protector of cities.

AQUINUM: A town in Latium, near Rome.

ARCHILOCHUS: Greek poet, who invented iambic verse.

ARGIVE: A Greek from the Peloponnesus region.

ARICIA: A town in Latium, not far from Rome.

ARISTARCHUS: Alexandrian grammarian and critic, second century B.C.E.

ARISTIPPUS: A philosopher from Cyrene, in North Africa.

ARMENIA: A region in Asia.

ATALLIDS: The name of a dynasty of kings in Mysia, in what is now Turkey.

ATREUS: King of Mycenae, father of Agamemnon and Menelaus and brother of Thyestes, whom he deceived into eating his own children.

ATTA: Titus Quinctius Atta, playwright, died 77 B.C.E. His name can suggest that he has a *vitium crurum*, something wrong with his legs, and therefore trouble managing his metrical feet. See "atta," *Oxford Latin Dictionary*.

AVENTINE: One of the seven hills of Rome.

BACCHUS: Roman name for Dionysus. God of wine, festivity, inspiration, and, in some contexts, moderation.

BAIAE: A fashionable resort on the Bay of Naples.

BRUNDISIUM: A seaport in Apulia, the port of embarkation for Greece and Asia. Its modern name is Brindisi.

CADMUS: Builder of Thebes. He and his wife, Harmonia, were turned into serpents.

CAECILIUS: G. Caecilius Statius, Roman comic poet, third century B.C.E.

CALABRIA: In modern times the name refers to the southwestern region of Italy, the toe of the boot; in ancient times it referred to the southeastern region, the heel of the boot.

CALLIMACHUS: Third century B.C.E. Greek poet.

CAMILLUS AND CURIUS: Heroes of earlier, Republican times, examples of plainer virtues.

CAMPUS MARTIUS: Fields in Rome where athletes exercised. The theater of Pompey was located there.

CANTABRIA: A region in the Iberian Peninsula. Agrippa was victorious there in 19 B.C.E.

CAPPADOCIA: A region in what is now Turkey.

CARINAE: A well-to-do residential section of Rome.

CASCELLIUS: Roman comic poet, second century B.C.E.

CASTOR AND POLLUX: Twin sons of Zeus (as a swan) and Leda, and brothers of Helen. Pollux was a great boxer. He and his brother Castor became the constellation Gemini, said to be able to bring calm to the waters.

CATO: Cato the Censor, second century B.C.E., who exemplified the austere values of the old Republic. Author of *De Agri Cultura*, which had important effects on Latin prose style.

CETHEGI: An ancient Roman family. In the old days they wore a sort of belted tunic instead of a toga.

CETHEGUS: Famous orator of the Republican era.

CHARYBDIS: Daughter of Poseidon and Gaea, sea and earth, who became a monstrous whirlpool off the coast of Italy.

CHOERILUS: Bad Greek poet, fourth century B.C.E.

CHREMES: A character in Terence's comedies.

CHRYSIPPUS: A third century B.C.E. Stoic philosopher.

CIRCE: The sorceress who turned Ulysses' men into swine and who bewitched and seduced Ulysses.

CIRCUS MAXIMUS: The great racetrack of Rome.

CLUSIUM: A town in Etruria, with baths nearby.

COLCHIANS: A people living near the Black Sea.

CRANTOR: A fourth century B.C.E. commentator on Plato.

CRATINUS: An Athenian comic poet.

CUMAE: A prosperous town and resort near Naples.

CYCLOPS: One-eyed giants, sons of Poseidon.

DELPHI: Site of the foremost oracle of Apollo.

DEMOCRITUS: Greek philosopher ("the laughing philosopher"), fifth century B.C.E.

DIANA: Goddess of the moon, of chastity, of the hunt, of childbirth.

DIGENTIA: The river near Horace's Sabine estate.

DIOMEDES: One of the greatest Greek heroes in the Trojan War. Son of Thyestes.

EMPEDOCLES: Fifth century B.C.E. Greek philosopher, born in Sicily.

ENNIUS: Second century B.C.E. Latin epic poet.

EPICHARMUS: Fifth century B.C.E. Sicilian comic playwright.

EUTRAPELUS: Publius Volumnius Eutrapelus, famous for scornful wit.

FABIANS: A prominent Roman family and their followers.

FALERNUM: A town in the Campania, near Rome, where the Falernian wine comes from.

FERENTINUM: A dreary town in the countryside near Rome.

GABII: A village and spa east of Rome; its tribe was allied with Rome in the fifth century B.C.E.

GAETULIA: A region of what is now Libya, in North Africa.

GARGANUS: A cape in southeastern Italy.

GRACCHUS: Tiberius Gracchus and his brother Gaius were celebrated orators.

HEBRUS: A river in Thrace.

HELICON: A mountain in Greece, home of the Muses and thus sacred to poetry.

HELLESPONT: The strait that runs from the Black Sea to the Aegean, dividing Europe from Asia.

HERCULES: Son of Zeus and Alcmena. Performed the Twelve Labors. Sometimes worshipped as a god, and in Horace's account he indeed became a god.

HEROD THE GREAT: King of Judaea (reigned 37–4 B.C.E.). The costly splendor of his court was celebrated.

HYDRA: A nine-headed serpent killed by Hercules.

IARBITAS: An imitator of Timagenes, a celebrated Alexandrian rhetorician, contemporary with Horace.

INO: Daughter of King Cadmus. Hera drove her mad and she leaped into the sea and became a sea deity.

IO: Daughter of a river god. Zeus turned her into a heifer to protect her from his wife, Hera. Io wandered the earth, pursued by a gadfly, and crossed the sea to Egypt. The Ionian Sea is named for her.

IXION: A murderous Thessalian king who fathered the race of Centaurs upon a cloud he thought was the goddess Hera. His punishment in the Underworld was to be bound on a wheel and whipped with serpents.

JANUS: God of doorways, crossroads, beginnings.

JANUS GATE: A gate in Rome which was closed when there was peace, open when there was war.

LATIUM: The region of Italy around Rome.

LAVERNA: Goddess of thieves.

LEPIDUS: Marcus Aemilius Lepidus, consul.

LIBER: Bacchus.

LIBRARY OF APOLLO: A library on the Palatine Hill, founded by Augustus.

LIVIUS: Lucius Andronicus Livius, third century B.C.E., tragic playwright and translator-adapter of Homer.

LOLLIUS: Marcus Lollius, consul, 21 B.C.E.

LUCANIA: A region in southern Italy.

LUCULLUS: Lucius Licinius Lucullus, Roman general, consul in 74 B.C.E.

LYNCEUS: One of the Argonauts.

LYSIPPUS: Greek sculptor in the time of Alexander the Great, fourth century B.C.E.

MAECENAS: Horace's great friend and patron, Augustus's adviser and confidant. Horace had been welcomed into the circle of Maecenas by Virgil.

MEDEA: The sorceress wife of Jason, she killed their children when Jason betrayed her love.

MENANDER: Fourth century B.C.E. Greek comic playwright.

MENELAUS: King of Sparta, Agamemnon's brother. He was Helen's husband.

MESSALLA: Famous statesman and orator, contemporary with Horace.

MILETUS: A city in Asia Minor.

MIMNERMUS: Seventh century B.C.E. Greek poet.

MINERVA: The Roman name of Athena, goddess of wisdom.

MINTURNAE: A town on the Via Appia, south of Rome.

MUCIUS: Several famous lawyers and judges were of the family Mucius Scaevola.

MUSA: Antonius Musa was Augustus's physician, and Horace's.

NAEVIUS: Gnaeus Naevius, third century B.C.E. playwright and poet.

NESTOR: One of the greatest leaders against the Trojans, as an old man.

NUMA: Numa Pompilius, second king of Rome.

ORESTES: Son of Agamemnon and Clytemnestra. He killed his mother and her lover Aegisthus, who had murdered his father.

ORPHEUS: Son of Apollo and Calliope. Eurydice's husband. The great musician whose music almost succeeded in bringing Eurydice back to the world of the living.

OSIRIS: Egyptian god of the Underworld.

PACUVIUS: Marcus Pacuvius, second century B.C.E. poet and playwright; Ennius's nephew.

PARIS: Seducer of Helen. One of the sons of Priam, king of Troy.

PAROS: An island in the Cyclades.

PELEUS: King of Thessaly, father of Achilles.

PENELOPE: Ulysses' faithful wife.

PENTHEUS: King of Thebes, in Euripides' *Bacchae*. He threatened a prisoner who was the god Dionysus in disguise and was torn to bits by the Bacchantes in retaliation.

PETRINUM: A town in Latium.

PHAEACIANS: Mythical rich inhabitants of the island of Corfu.

PHILIPPI: The scene of the battle in which Brutus and Cassius were defeated by Octavian (later Augustus), 42 B.C.E.

PHRAATES: He usurped the Parthian throne in 37 B.C.E., lost it, and then regained it.

PINDAR: The sixth-century B.C.E. Greek poet.

PLAUTUS: Roman comic playwright, late third to second century B.C.E.

PONTIFFS: Priests of the state religion, advisers to the chief magistrate.

PRAENESTE: A mountain town near Rome, now called Palestrina.

PROCNE: When Tereus, the king of Thrace, assaulted Philomela, the sister of Procne, his wife, Philomela, and Procne took their revenge by killing Itylus, the child of Procne and Tereus, and serving him to Tereus for dinner. Philomela was turned into a nightingale, Tereus into a hoopoe, and Procne into a swallow.

PROTEUS: A shape-shifting sea god.

PUNIC: Carthaginian.

PYTHAGORAS: Mathematician and philosopher of the sixth century B.C.E. He encouraged belief in reincarnation.

QUINTILIUS: Quintilius Varus, a friend of Horace and Virgil. Horace praises him as a judicious critic.

QUIRINAL: One of the hills of Rome.

RHODES: A large island off the coast of Asia Minor.

ROSCIUS: Gallus Roscius, first century B.C.E. comic and tragic actor.

SABINES: A people who inhabited the region around Horace's estate; they became full Roman citizens in the third century B.C.E.

SALERNO: A town, now a city, on the coast south of Naples.

SAMNITES: A tribe in southern Italy, "primitive and warlike," according to the Oxford Classical Dictionary.

SAPPHO: The great poet. She was born on the island of Lesbos.

SCYLLA: A sea-nymph turned by jealous Circe, in Homer's Odyssey, into dangerous rocks opposite the whirlpool Charybdis, in the strait between Italy and Sicily.

SIRENS: Sister sea-nymphs, in the Odyssey, who tried, by singing, to lure Ulysses and his shipmates toward the rocky shore and disaster.

SOPHOCLES: Greek tragic poet, fifth century B.C.E.

SORRENTO: A town on the Bay of Naples. Its ancient name was Surrentum.

STATILIUS TAURUS: Consul, 26 B.C.E.

STERTINIUS: A Roman contemporary of Horace, who wrote verses summarizing Stoic doctrine.

SYLVANUS: A god of the woods.

TARENTUM: A city in Apulia near Horace's birthplace. Its modern name is Taranto.

TARPA: Maecius Tarpa, mentioned by Cicero as a critic of plays.

TEANUM: A hillside resort town in Campania.

TELEMACHUS: Son of Ulysses.

TELEPHUS: The subject of a tragedy by Euripides.

TELLUS: Goddess of earth, soil.

TEN MEN: The *decemviri*, patricians appointed (fifth century B.C.E.) to codify Roman laws.

TERENCE: Publius Terentius Afer, second century B.C.E. comic playwright.

THEBES: A Greek city, in the Boeotian region.

THEON: Traditional name for a slanderer.

THESPIS: Greek tragic poet, sixth century B.C.E.

THESSALY: A region of northern Greece.

THRACE: The vast region which is now northeastern Greece and southern Bulgaria.

THYESTES: Brother of Atreus, king of Mycenae, who tricked him into eating his own children.

TIBERIUS: Tiberius Claudius Nero Caesar, Augustus's stepson and successor.

TIBULLUS: Albius Tibullus, the elegiac poet, was born in 49 B.C.E. and died in 19 B.C.E.

TIBUR: The ancient name for Tivoli, a town near Horace's Sabine estate, outside Rome.

TIMAGENES: Greek rhetorician famous for his style.

TYRTAEUS: Greek poet of the seventh century B.C.E.

ULYSSES: Odysseus, one of the great leaders of the Greeks against the Trojans and the hero of Homer's *Odyssey*, the story of his long voyage home after the Trojan War.

VACUNA: A rural Sabine deity.

VARIUS: Lucius Varius Rufus, a dramatist and writer of epic poetry, very much admired by both Virgil and Horace.

VELIA: A seaside town in Lucania, south of Naples.

VELINI: A Roman tribe.

VICOVARO: Modern name of the nearest town to Horace's Sabine farm; its ancient name was Varia.

Printed in the USA
CPSIA information can be obtained
at www.ICGtesting.com
LVHW091132150724
785511LV00001B/97